Like Water
(A Haiku Collection)

Like Water
(A Haiku Collection)

Keiselim A. Montás

Translated by Elizabeth Polli

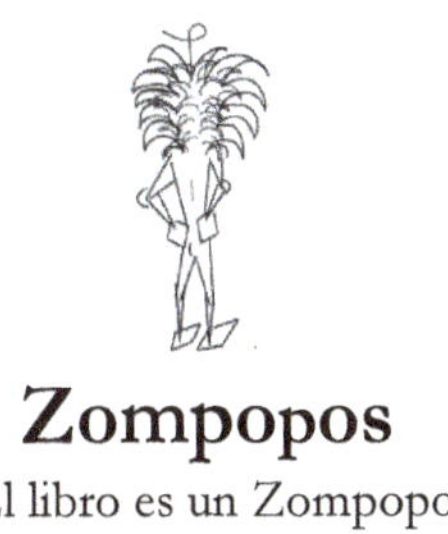

Zompopos
El libro es un Zompopo

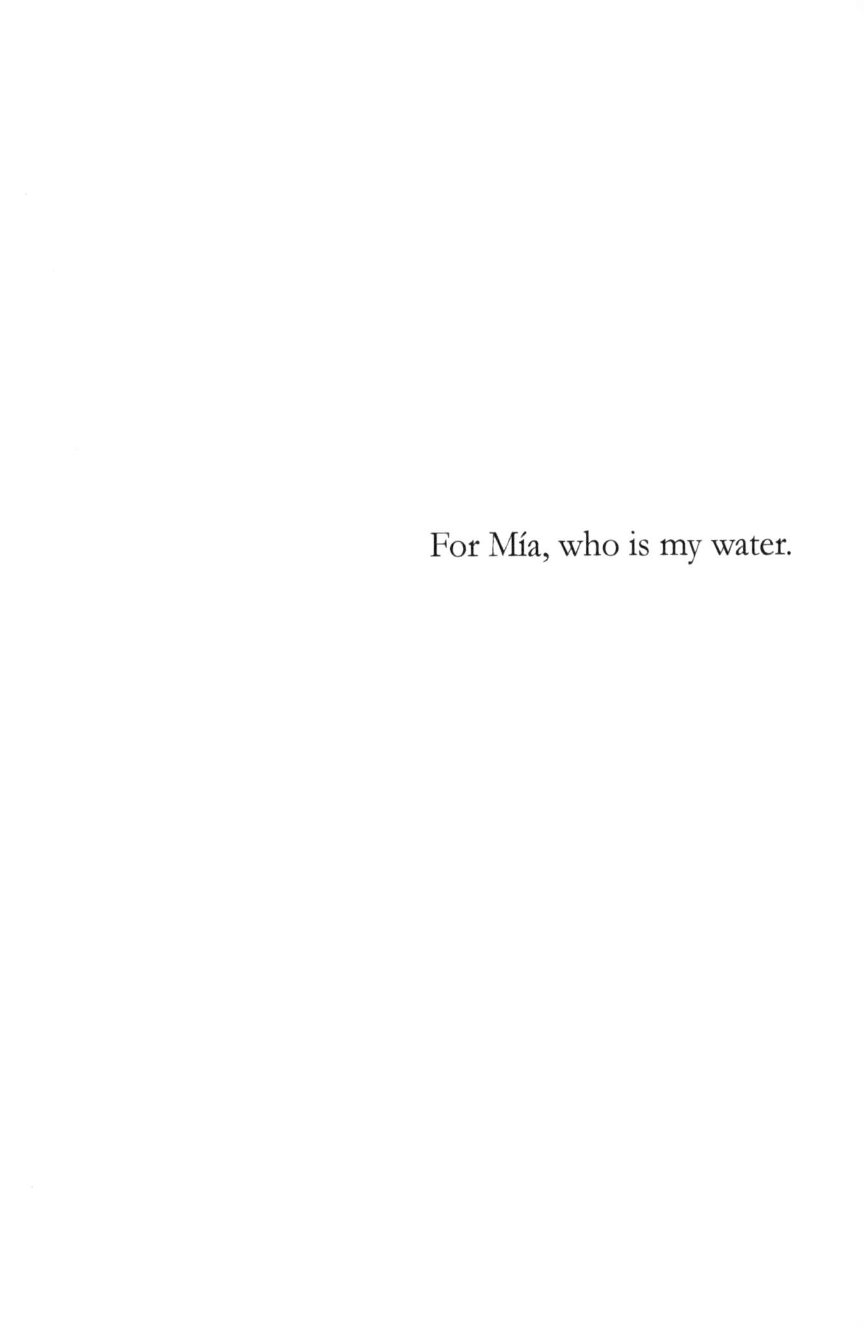

For Mía, who is my water.

Contents

Foreword   xi

Preface   xiii

Acknowledgments   xv

Introduction   1

Water（水）   5
   漁夫 (fisherman)
   筏 (raft)
   せせらぎ (stream)
   海 (sea)
   雨 (rain)
   川 (river)
   凍てついたせせらぎ (frozen brook)
   逢引 (date)
   水循環 (water cycle)
   舞 (dance)
   雪解け水 (melting ice/snow)

Nature (自然) 19

蛍 (firefly)

夜明け (day break)

鳥居 (torii)

夏 (summer)

冬 (winter)

極光 (dawn)

春 (spring)

砂漠 (desert)

竹 (bamboo)

楓 (maple)

虹 (rainbow)

蜱 (tick)

胡蝶 (butterfly)

木 (tree)

発芽 (germination)

フレーム (frame)

Life （人生）

- 弓道　(archery)
- 対　(versus)
- 誕生　(birth)
- 井戸　(well)
- 茶道　(tea ceremony)
- 糸　(thread)
- 忘却　(oblivion)
- 生命　(life)
- 凧　(kite)
- 信条　(creed)
- 時間　(time)
- 出発　(departure)
- 人間　(human being)
- 調和　(harmony)
- 仮出獄　(probation)

Writing （書） 61

最後の詩 (last verse)
待合室 (waiting room)
不完全 (imperfection)
劇作家 (playwright)
憂鬱 (melancholy)
掛け軸 (*kakejiku*: vertical roll of caligraphy)
真髄 (essential)

Translator's Note 73

Foreword

ATOMS IN THE SHAPE OF POEMS

It would seem that Keiselim searches within the breath of the haiku for the essence of nature. His poetry collection *Like Water* is a diary of images and miniature verses. They are condensed atoms that sketch the shape of the briefest of moments.

An extreme smallness that explodes and expands. Fish become enormous in the water while the fisherman turns into a furtive earthworm.

The secret of atoms in the shape of poems lies within the ability that Keiselim has to evoke landscapes brought to fruition in each verse. He recreates in them a simple dance of images that are arranged in verses of five, seven and five syllables.

The art of the haiku is revived in the fleeting glance, which breathes in everything, and turns into a twinkle of light and sky. A red bridge that crosses over streams, that listens to the coursing water and grows into a sailboat made of salt, into foam that balances on the edge of rocks.

Keiselim presents the calendar to us and leads us by the hand through images of time: rainy spring days, autumn and its dry leaves, a blanket of snow and bare trees. Keiselim listens patiently to the voice of water, with its roar, its murmur and its echo. The water speaks to the poet; it's a liquid language that carries him to the ocean of life.

The poet of water searches as well for a space in nature in which to describe the night and the dawn. Vegetation found in corners grows on, changing its tone. The bareness of the tree trunks is covered with the density of a cottony chill.

Keiselim is obsessed with frozen time that thickens in wintertime. In his haiku the ritual of the naked tree is explained, the voracity of ticks embedded in skin or the metamorphosis of worms that dream of becoming butterflies.

Nature, writing and life are rivers of fullness-in-love that carry along shadows and gestures. They are drops of light that burst into images and evoke other realities. They are like the trunk that grows and transforms itself into the inspirations of small cities.

The cycle of life is sketched in images, with its all-absorbing seeds and thoughts. Everything is traced out in Keiselim's imaginary. Everything lives within the language of his poetic expressions, and Elizabeth Polli translates them, so that Keiselim can speak to us twice over.

The path of words lies gathered in verses. The path of bare feet that travel the world over. The path of the confused God that took refuge in poetry. Words inhabit Keiselim's soul. Words that draw for us a calendar of dreams. Words of rain that feed every horizon. Atoms that grow with each new reading. Atoms of love that find their essence in words, in a rainbow or in a butterfly.

Ana Merino

Preface

I have chosen to adhere to a traditional notion of haiku, in that I prefer 3 verses, in 5/7/5 format for a total of 17 syllables; and, whenever possible, the use of a *kigo* (季語) or season word. However, I do sometimes diverge, particularly when the poem takes on a more philosophical tone (which is not necessarily a haiku theme), and part of that divergence from tradition is the introduction of a subtitle for each poem.

To the reader, thus, I owe this short preface: I chose to include a subtitle in Japanese for each poem, as a way of honoring and thanking the Japanese culture for the gift of haiku, and as a way of honoring my journey to this exquisite poetic form.

Spanish is my first and native language. I read and wrote my first haiku in English. Over the years, my interest in Japanese culture and poetry grew, and I have done most of my readings in Spanish; subsequently my haiku writing has happened in Spanish.

Considering that this poetic form came to me, one can say, in translation; or better yet, it came to me as the words come to one watching a foreign film: in subtitles; I am reversing that process of translation in thrice over (English, Spanish, Japanese), by adding a subtile to each poem. The subtitles aim at capturing the central idea of each poem, much in the way a title would, but in Japanese; doing so here, makes it function as the subtiltles in foreign films do, but reversed.

The table of contents has, in turn, English translations of the "subtitles" and by providing the translation in the table of contents only, I am inviting the reader to be part of this linguistic journey that has brought me to bring you this collection of haiku.

¡Gracias por leerme!

Thank you for reading!

この本をお手に取って下さった方々に感謝いたします

Keiselim A. Montás

Acknowledgments

Special thanks go to Sachi Schmidt-Hori, for her revision of the Japanese subtitles and for her subtle suggestions; also to Elena Hikari " 光 " and Akiko Harimoto "Soja" (both from *Shodo Creativo*) for their art.

And a heartfelt thank you (profundo agradecimiento) to Andy Castillo, for his paintbrush, his pencil, his talent and his friendship; because his illustrations flow like a rain shower over Caribbean tin roofs, like ink over *washi* (和紙), and like snowflakes flying among the leafless birch trees in my backyard.

Introduction

LIKE WATER: A VAST CONCISION*

Water at the beginning and at the end: two doors that open and close throughout this book of poems by Keiselim A. Montás, forging a vast concatenation; water garlands that end up being an eternal return, cyclical vision of nature, life and writing through the path of water. The title functions like a simile (that is: like writing and like incentive of continuity in the writing) and, at the same time, like a foundation for the understanding and retention of one of the four elements (water) that makes up reality from the perspective of Western tradition: water, which "like water," in its different moments, has three that this book privileges: its flowing (where flowing implies modulation and Heraclitean change, implies obstruction and drifting); its stagnation (and nature here, halted, can be reflected in a contemplative and auto-reflexive act); and, its ultimate moment of finding the sea (which is at the same time a natural occurrence, a philosophical concept and a personal narration of the poet faced with the inevitable: "our lives are the rivers / that end up at the sea / which is death").

Water tends to overflow, the universal deluge (catastrophic) is one of its everyday possibilities, recurrent, at the same time historically mythologized, universally told and retold in numerous traditions, and likewise interiorized in all universal poetry as a sign of devastation and death: and of resurrection and continuity. The poet has the option of the overflow, or the occasion (chosen by Montás' conception) of

1

restraint: the haiku, which is not utilized systematically throughout this work by whim but rather as a weapon of correction that rectifies reality and moderates language; it's the poetic mechanism (and not gratuitous in the least), which, in this case, is used for the purpose of coordinating the abrupt changes we are subjected to by water. Water that overflows has a dike in the haiku, not a chute but a limit, not muddled but limpid; and from that simple and quick clarity of this form of expression, a fulcrum that unites and reunites the diverse elements of nature, of living reality and its writing, in an inviting space in which all creatures have their necessary place (the function of the poet rests on discovering and revealing it). A place where, throughout the entire collection, a harmonious relationship persists between subject and object, between nature and writing, between life and the sensation of life.

The haste of existence leads to the separation between subject and object; yet, the brevity which characterizes the haiku (brush stroke, paper, intuition, gesture and act of inscription, conjunction and swift ending) gives back the union between subject and object to existence. It does so in such a manner that, while everything flows, diverts, and seeks out its path (of perfection), everything at the same time turns into unity, into mutual participation, into a living relationship. In this way, "Whilst man is cane rod / on top of the raft —earthworm— / the fish is water." The earthworm is not a symbol of anything, it is not a sign of human suffering, nor any kind of transference; the earthworm is the earthworm, and in this case its function is being bait, a natural function that has its logic, vehicle of conjunction between poet and poem, between the need for expression (which is a need for comprehension), and an outcome: the haiku of a book which like water, springs up, moves, stops, continues, forges realities, establishes adjustments and readjustments (as it happens with all paths), and ends at its sea. It is not by chance that the title contains water, nor that the first and last poems of the book end up, with diverse meanings, with water.

A referential book which demands of the reader a certain knowledge, and a search for anchor points for a better understanding of the text. Where there is a breast stroke in water that crosses to the other side, we have, for example, a hidden and valid reference to the Heart Sutra and its *gate gate paragate parasamgate bodhi swaha*. In the haiku with the "Coursing of water," the poetic speaker is found facing change, thus giving the poem a Heraclitean meaning, one of the strong signs of historical thought, intermingled with Western and Eastern tonalities, in such a way that Heraclitus serves as bridge, as torii, to two cultures that we have always thought of as separate, contrasting them as opposites, and that now, finally, we try to understand as part of the same complex and plural vision of Humanity. Or, fireflies that flutter in the dark night, and give off their own light, might refer to either "The Dark Night" of San Juan de la Cruz, or to Nature as used in the poetry of Bashō.

Like Water is a delicate tapestry of words and images, a foliage that turns green, dries out, dies and reappears as in natural seasons with deft and concise language. Centered in a mental and physiological eye that seeks, without exasperation or haste, the greatest possible understanding of that which, day by day, is present in front of us. Poem by poem, page by page, the elements concatenate, intertwine and exchange fundamentals, to break with sealed compartments and vicious circles, and to create in their place that beautiful "to and fro of rocks" of one of the first poems in the book. We are in front of a work where everything, in harmony, is sequence, consequence, continuity: Heraclitus holding hands with Parmenides, that which flows embraces that which remains. There is no enmity but understanding, there is no harm but gentle cauterizing and reparation.

Carpentry, architecture, vision. The seasons centered, one by one, in sisterhood concentrated through the focus of the eye and the hand of the poet. Water retained and water that flows, water that is water and that is like water. Everything is connected and can have the luxury of being vapor, fog and haze, ascend and descend, fall and jolt, and restoration. And in all this process (swift and endless, mirror and mirage of nature), language is at the service of poetic creation, and it flows like water flows to end up in a beautiful book of poems from the hands of the Dominican poet Keiselim A. Montás. He has, at the same time, been able to conjugate writing with painting; his own alphabet with another's alphabet; ulterior beauty from the proximity of the moment, its initial sparkling and its long path to the most still and pure light of a geography of frozen sands; and a personal and universal architecture, where from humility, "The cold naked trees, / in February, dream of / blossoming springtime."

José Kozer

This Introduction was translated by Keiselim A. Montás from the Prologue to the original Spanish version of the book.

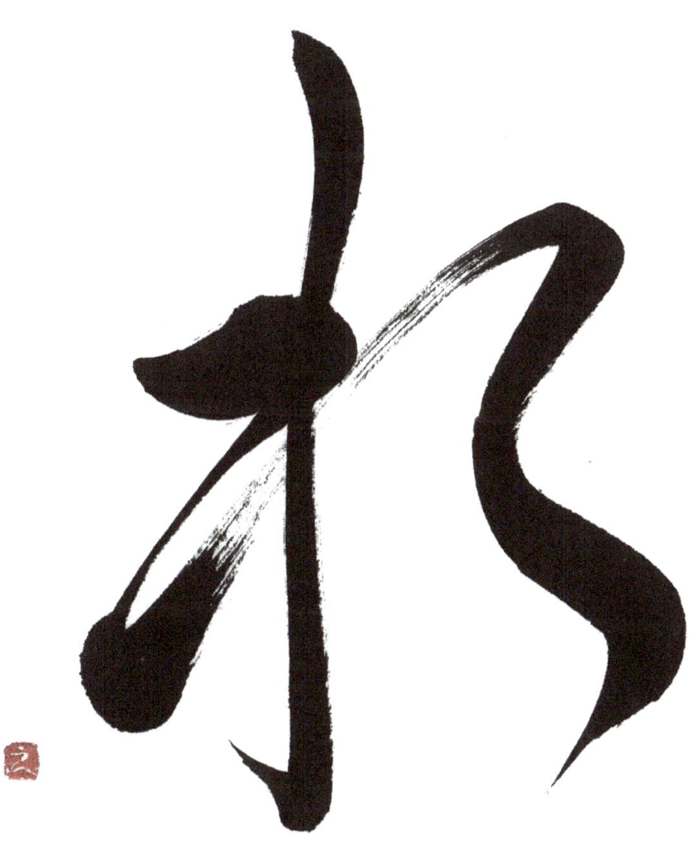

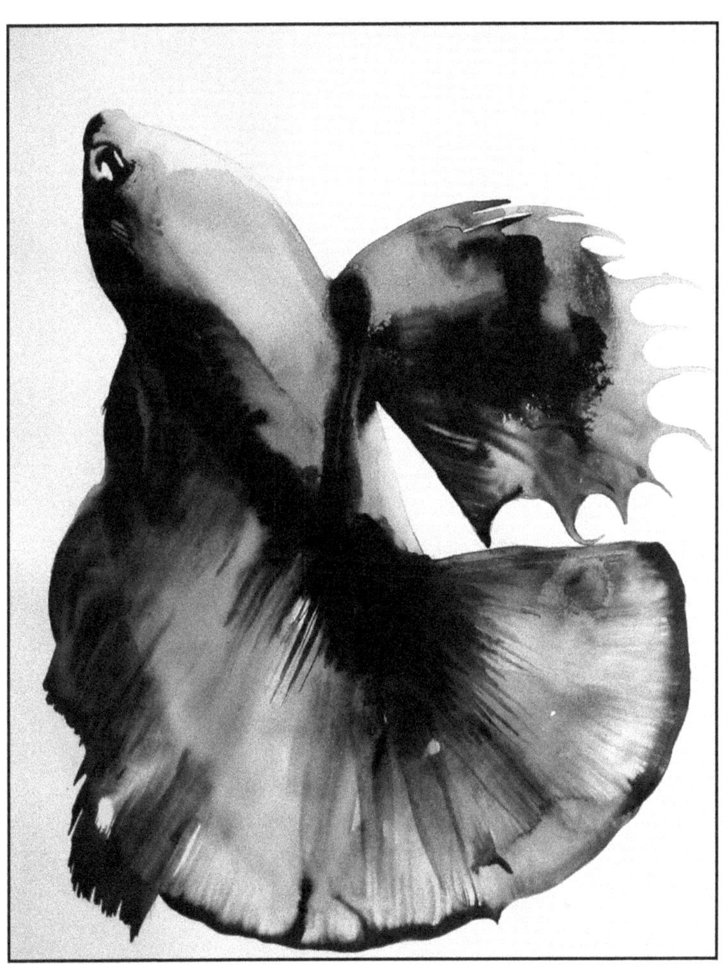

Whilst man is cane rod
on top of the raft —earthworm—
the fish is water.

漁夫

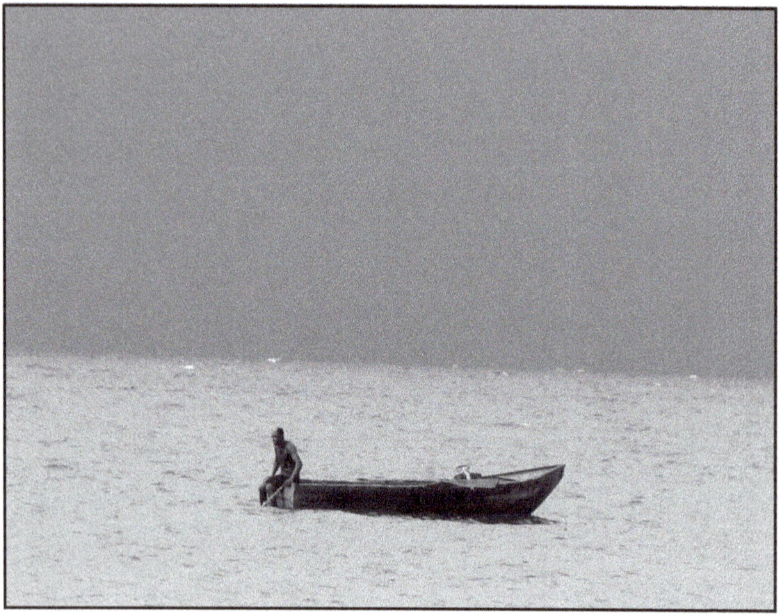

Breast stroke in water
wing that crosses —lightning fast—
to the other side.

筏

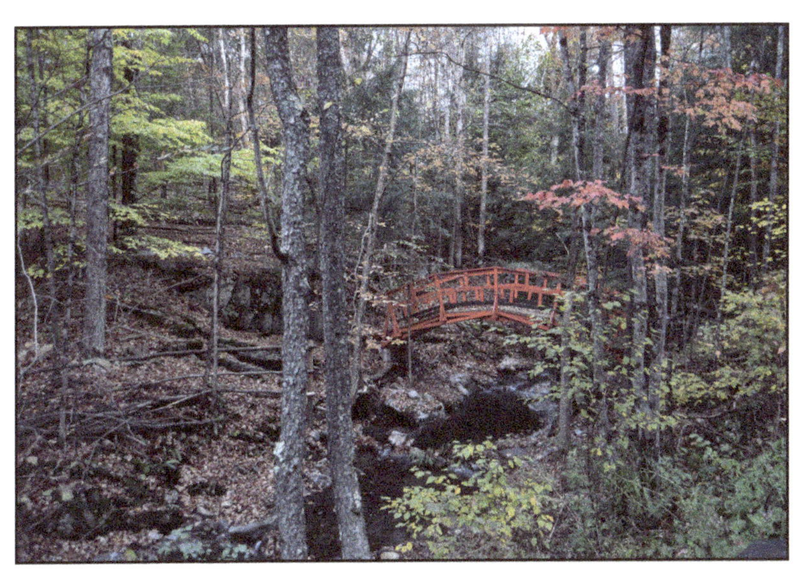

Leafage and heavens,
a bridge over the river:
coursing of waters.

せせらぎ

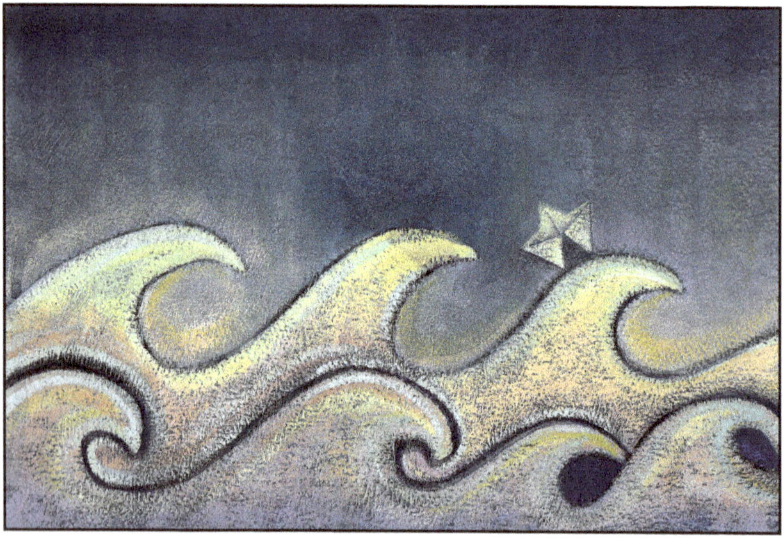

Sailing boat of salt
journeys into winds of foam;
to and fro of rocks.

海

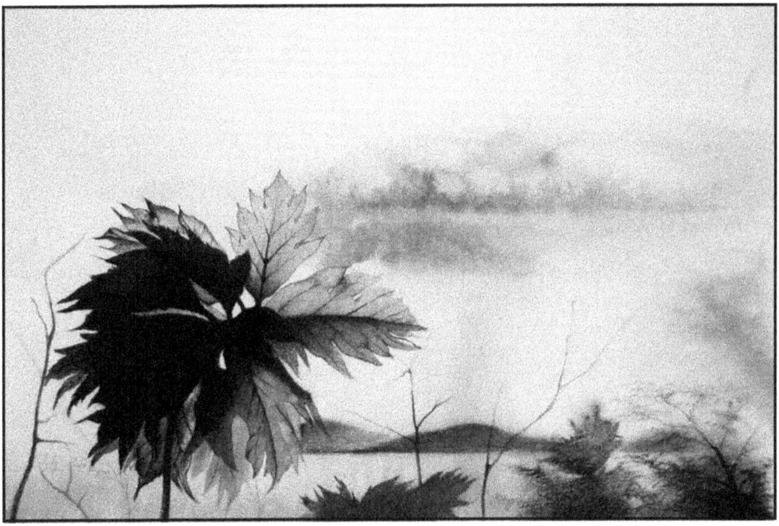

The rains of autumn
remove the leaves that are placed
by rains of April.

雨

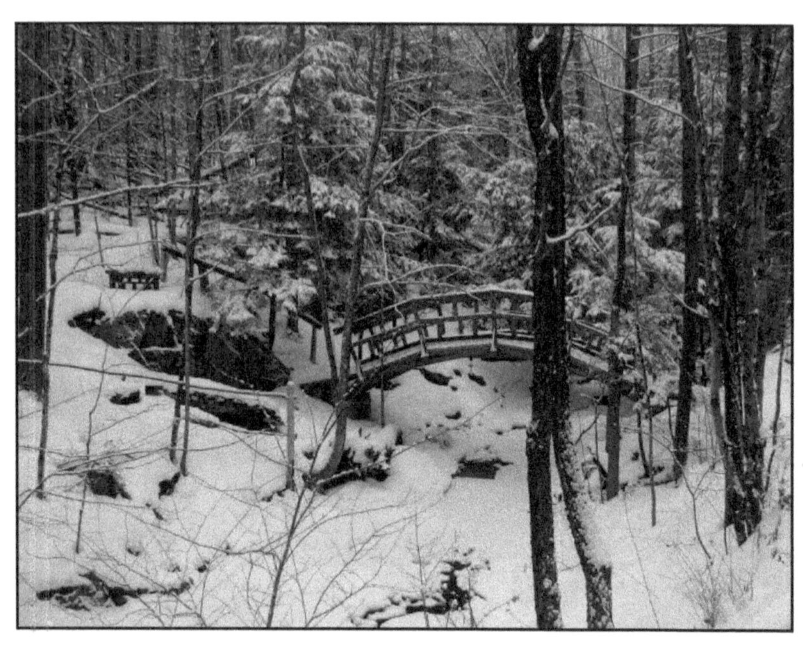

Coursing of water,
you change; I recognize you,
you're the very same.

川

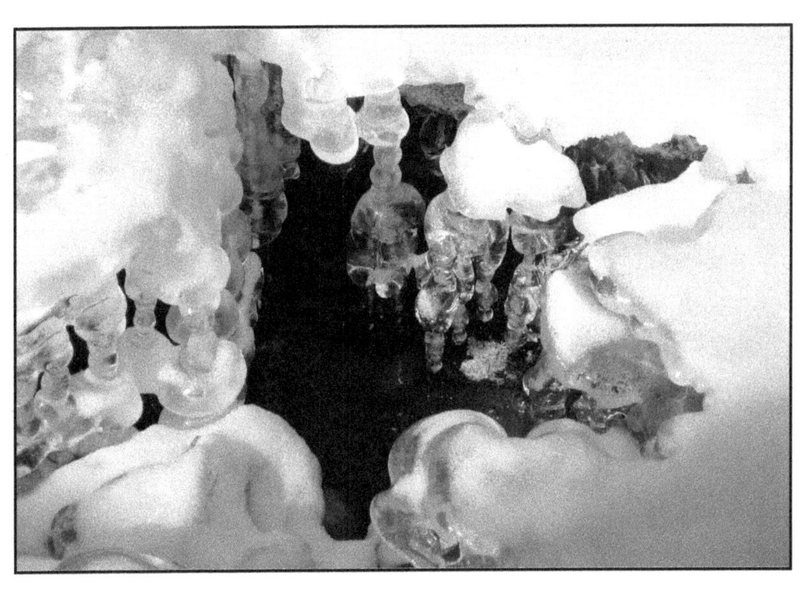

Roaring of April
—the murmuring of August—
wintertime echo.

凍てついたせせらぎ

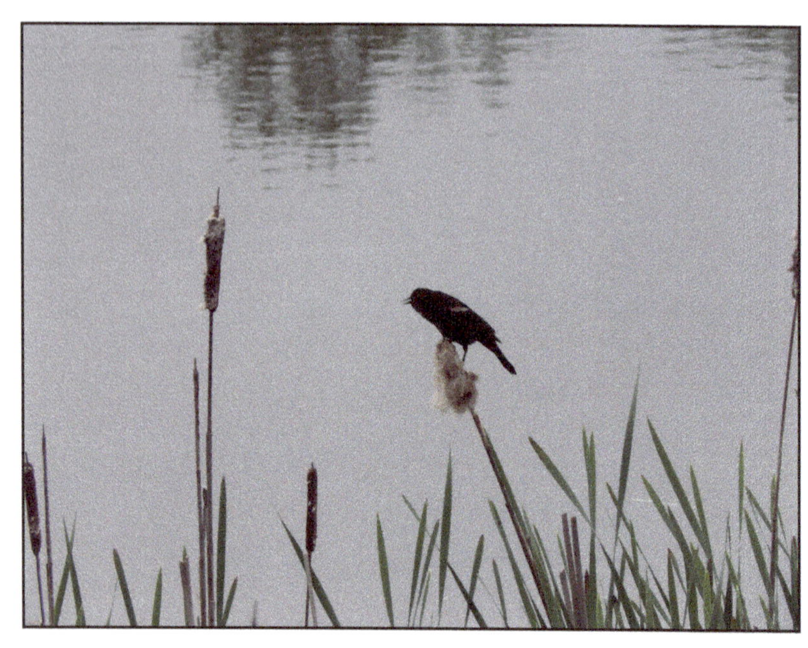

A smiling female
—river's reflection— because
a male casts a wink.

逢引

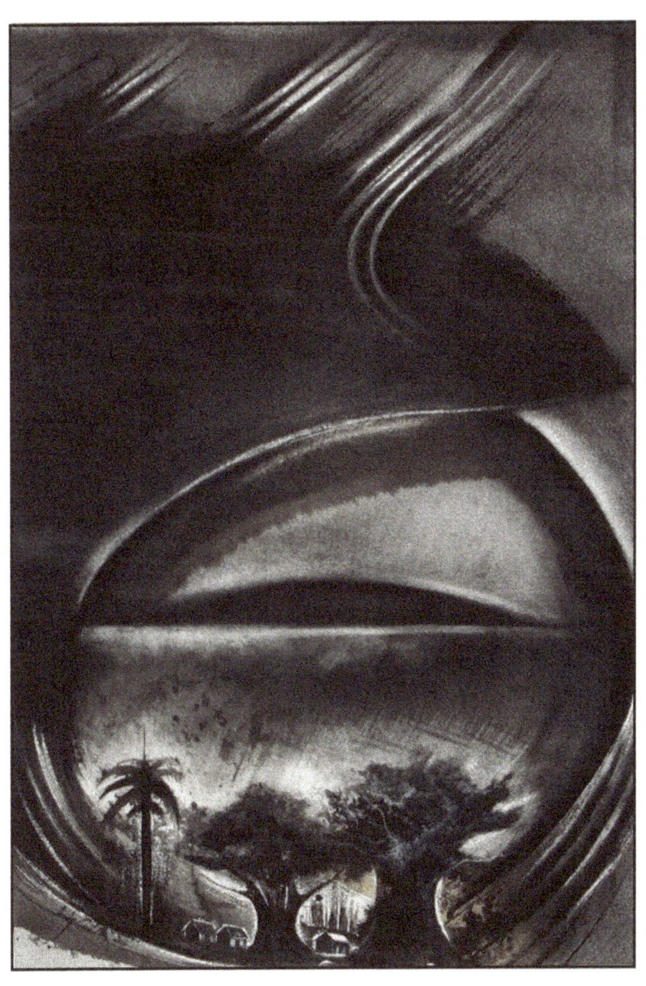

It soars as vapor
swiftly, to a high repose:
it descends in clumps.

水循環

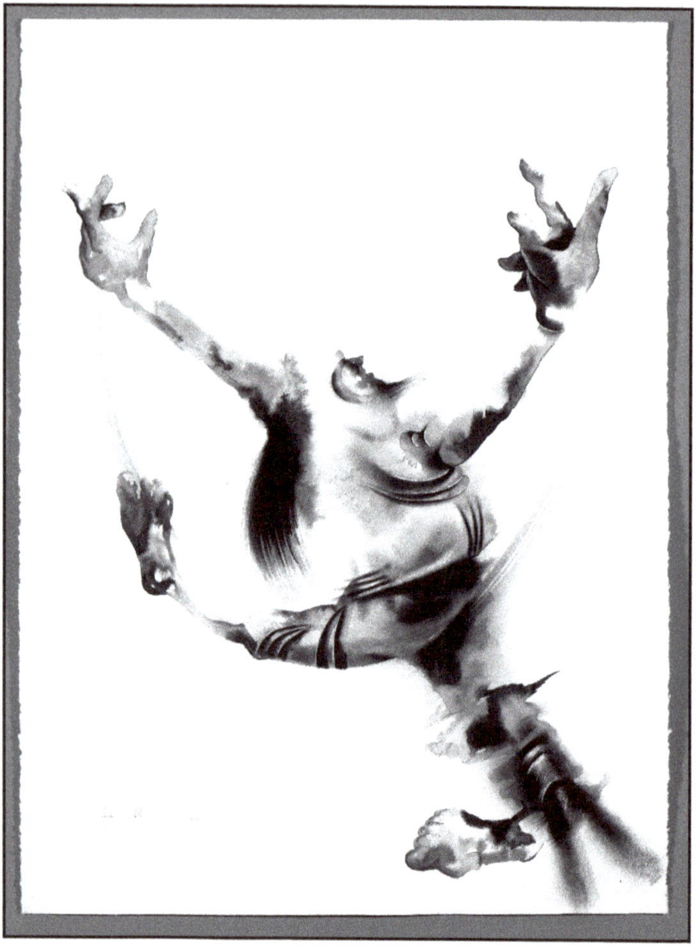

Snow flurries in March;
waltz of departing winter
and arriving spring.

舞

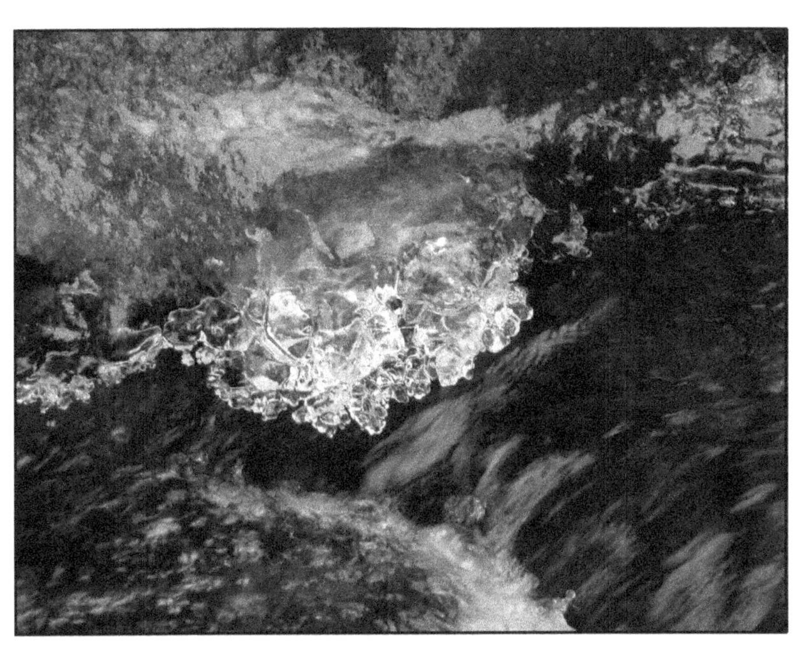

Crystal fluid state
in the purring sound that flows
en route to April.

雪解け水

Nature

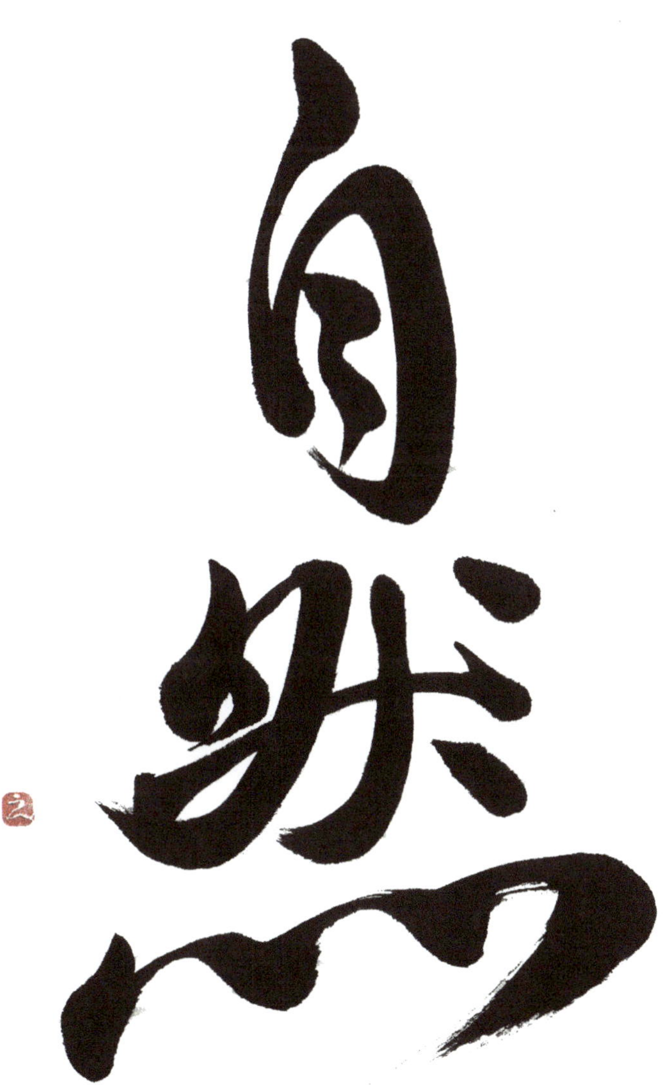

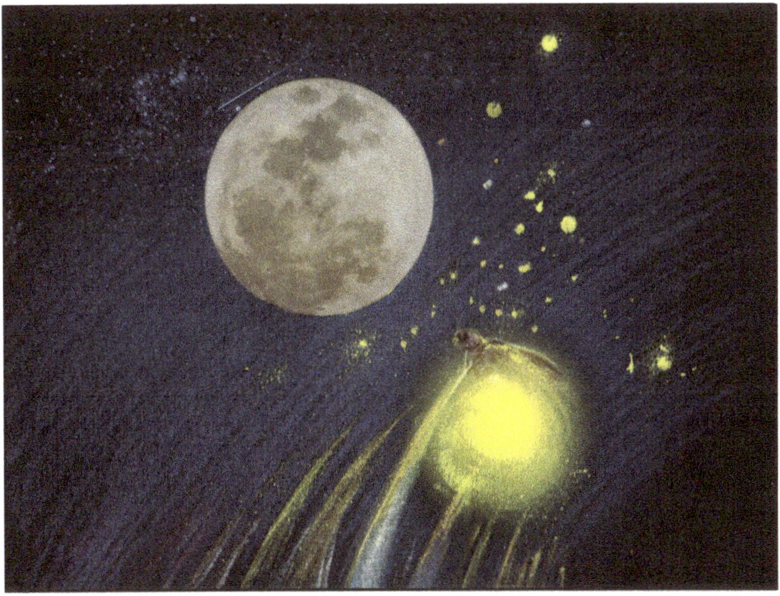

There are those fireflies,
that on the darkest of nights
flutter as though lights.

蛍

21

The sun undressing
mountains of garments tailored
by the morning fog.

夜明け

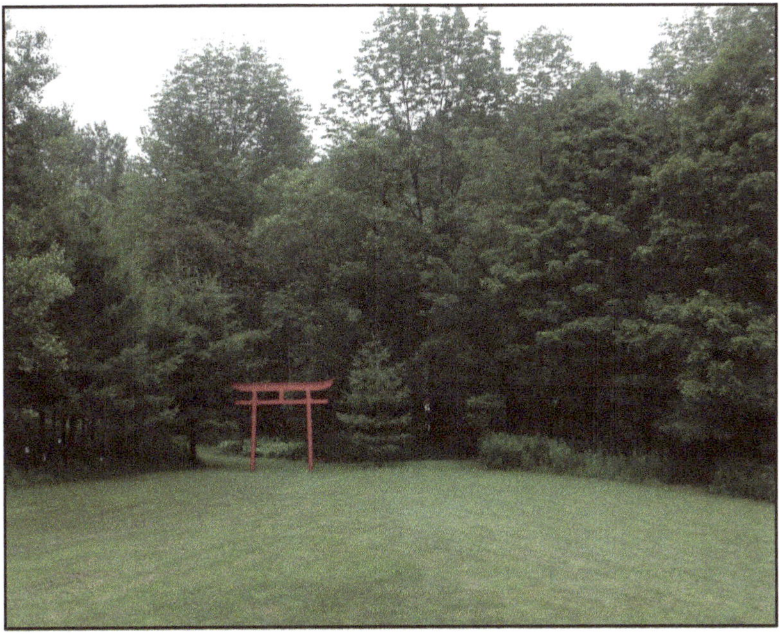

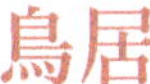

The yard's green background
gives way —passage— as Torii,
to wide-open red.

鳥居

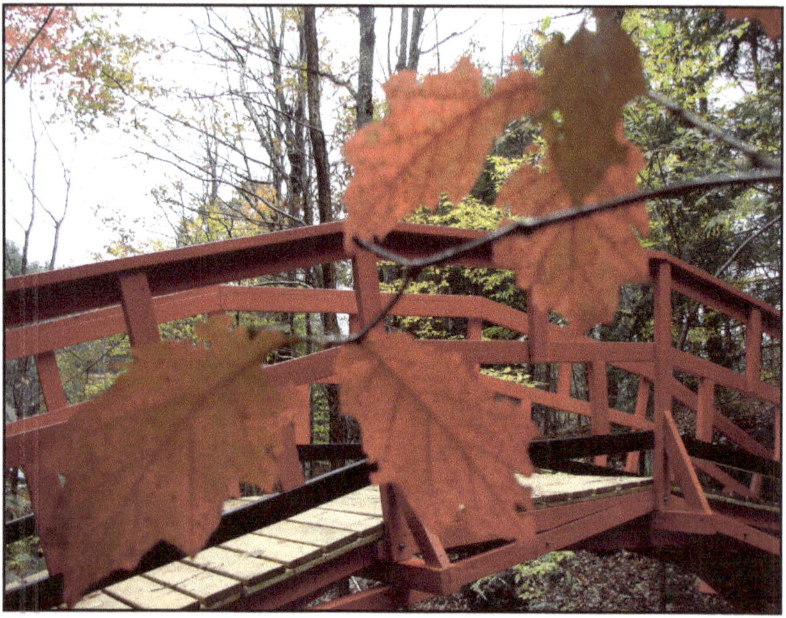

April is verdant
—summertime is a bridge—and
October blushes.

夏

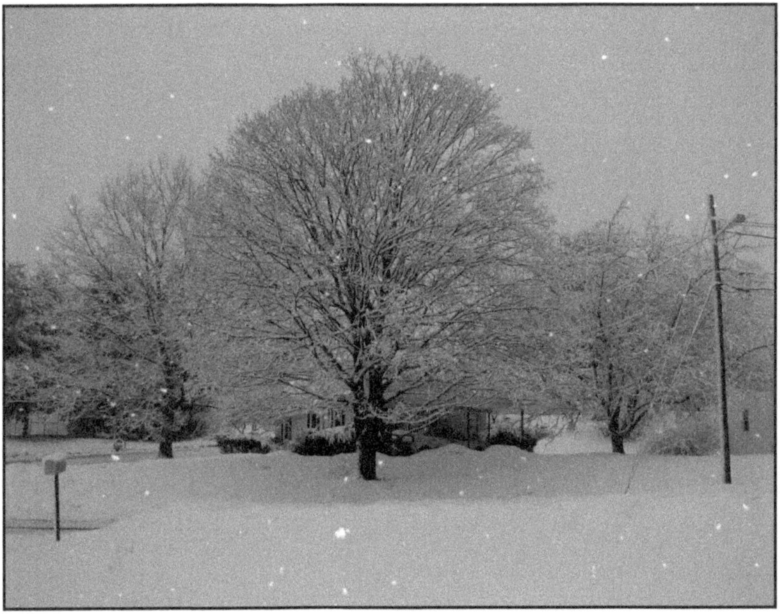

The snow, like cotton,
(garment for the skeleton)
has covered the tree.

冬

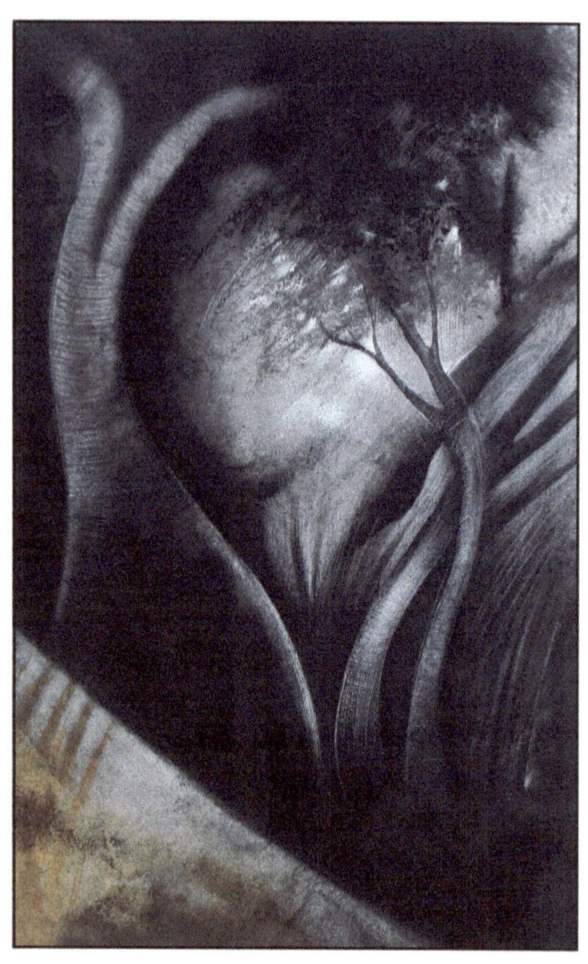

And it's from the night
—after slow hours concluded—
that the day is born.

極光

26

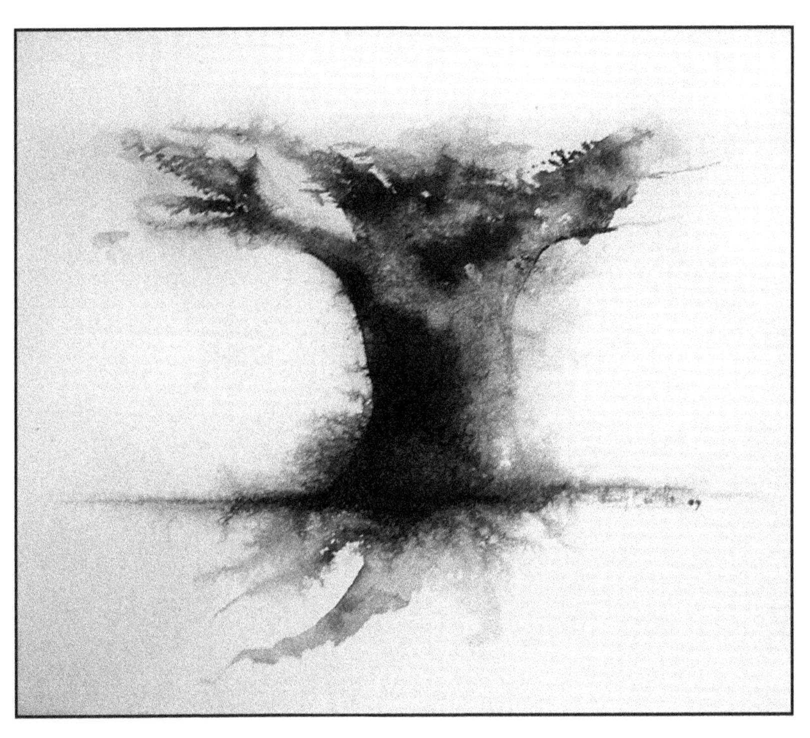

The cold naked trees,
in February, dream of
blossoming springtime.

春

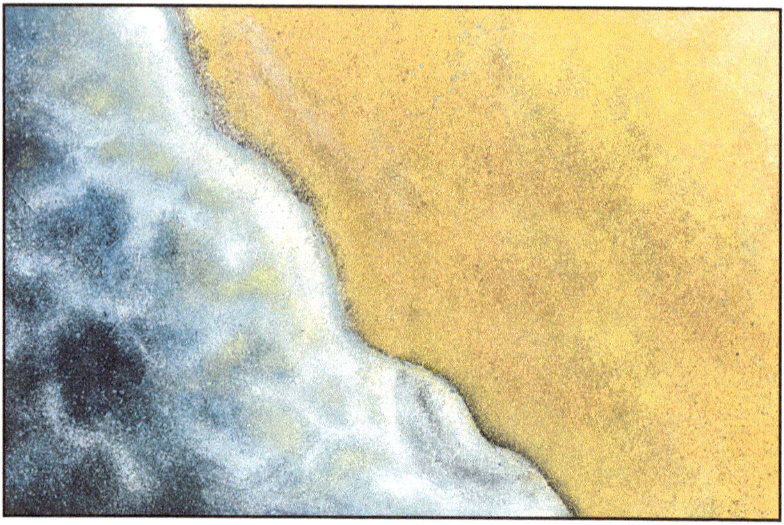

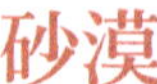

The expansive sands
—days of constant inferno—
of bone-chilling nights.

砂漠

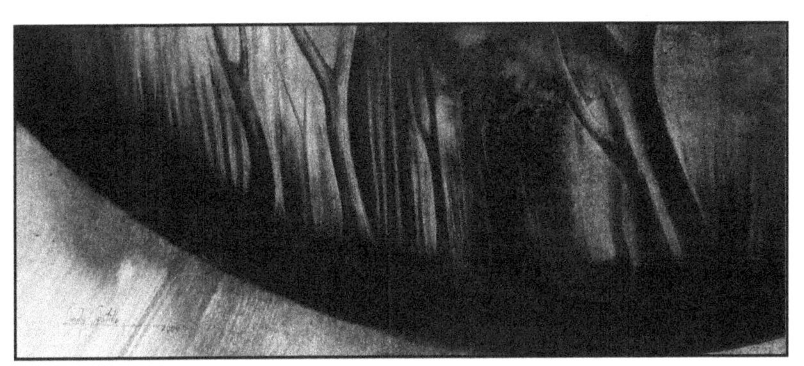

Path in the forest
delineating the route
in tall green bamboo.

竹

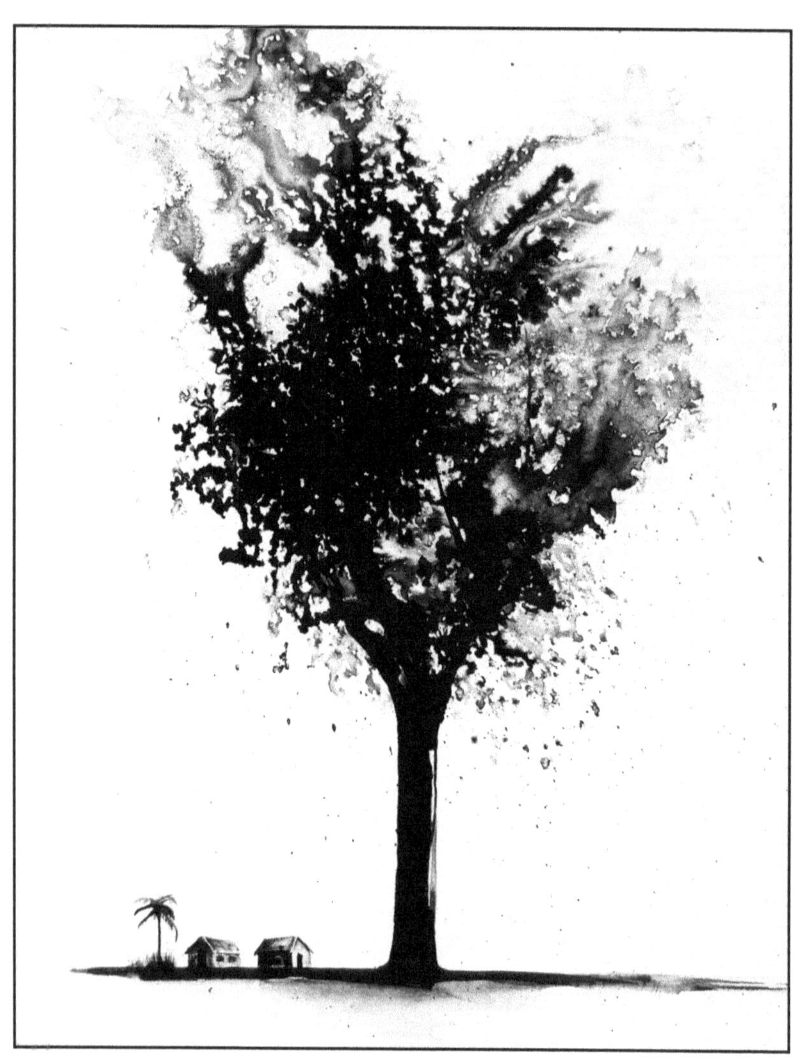

The undressing of
autumn dresses yet again
a blossoming spring.

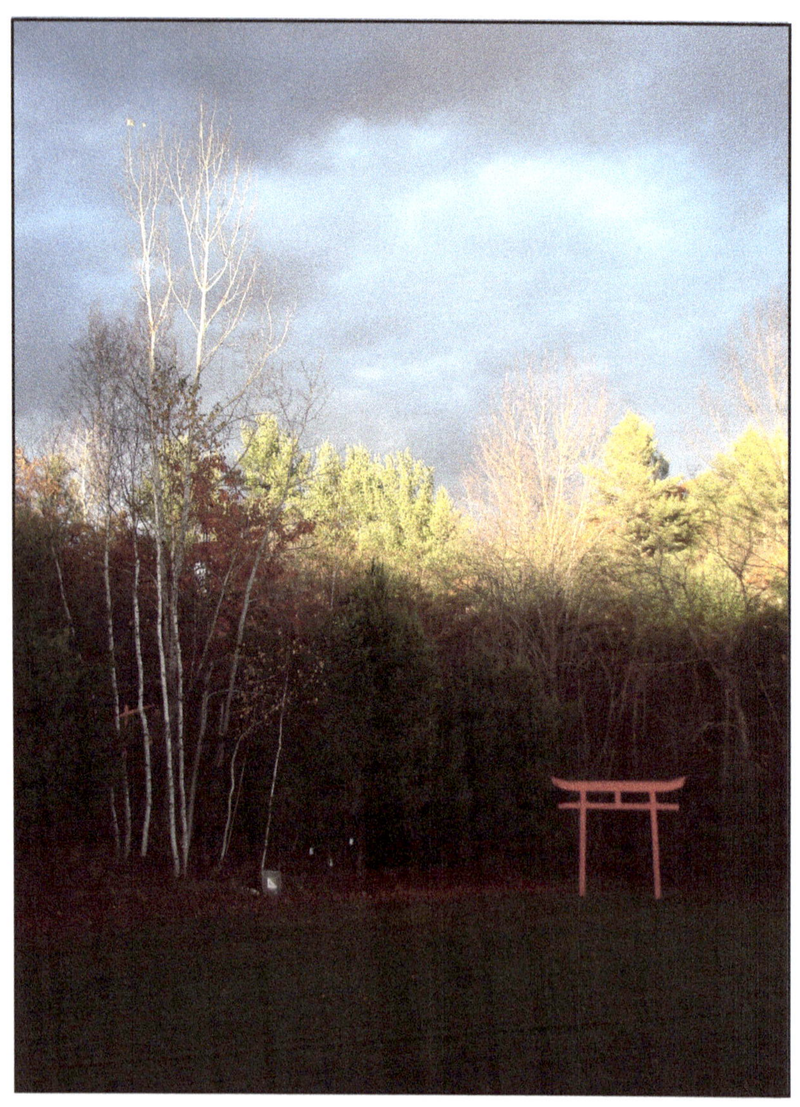

Seven colorings
—arching— a bridge connecting
the earth and the sky.

虹

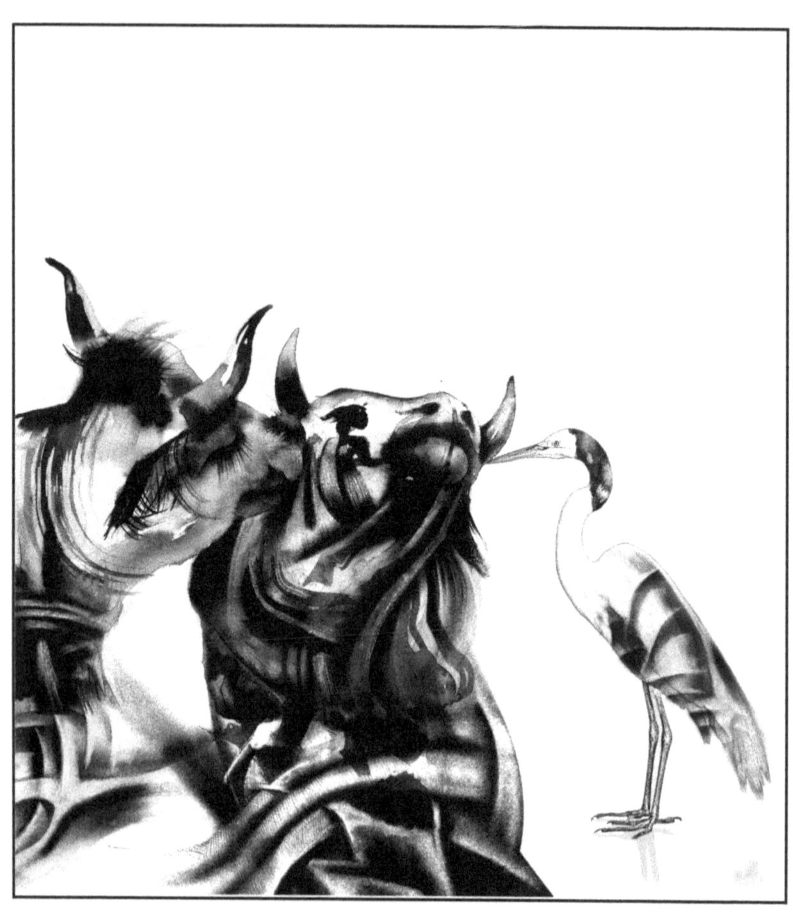

The heron, the cow
—are united and yet not—
by the cussed tick.

蜱

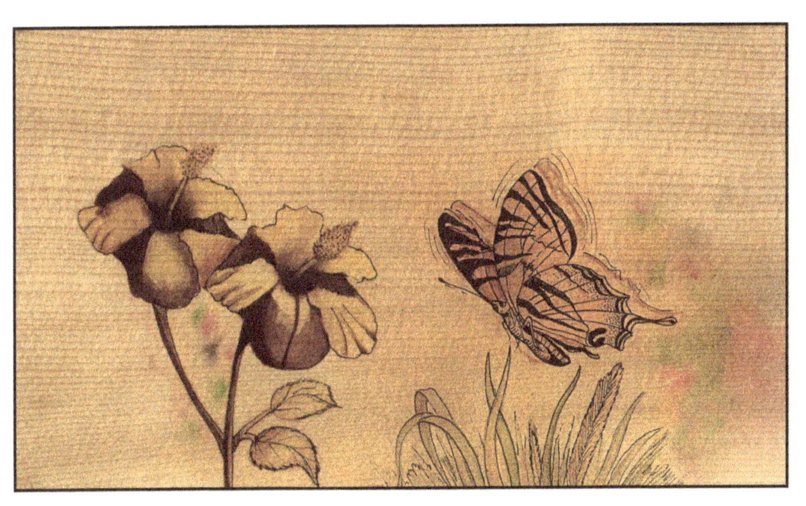

From the chrysalis
(the silkworm itself); and now:
wings break out for flight.

胡蝶

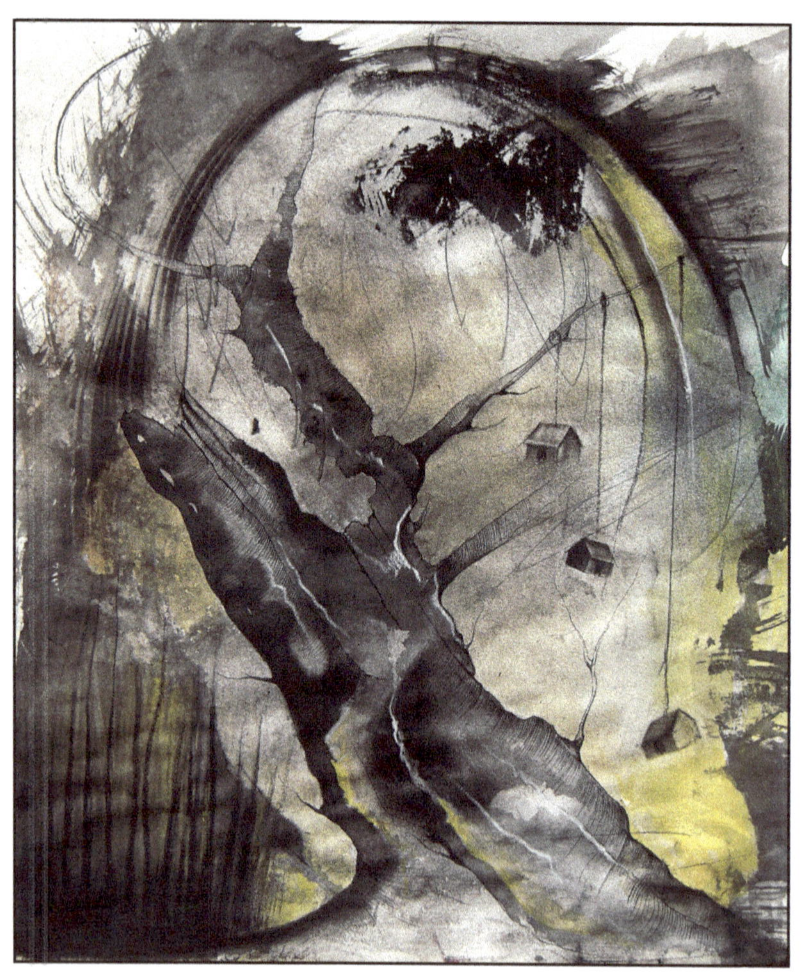

The trunks of wild trees
thicken to turn into house,
rowboat or charcoal.

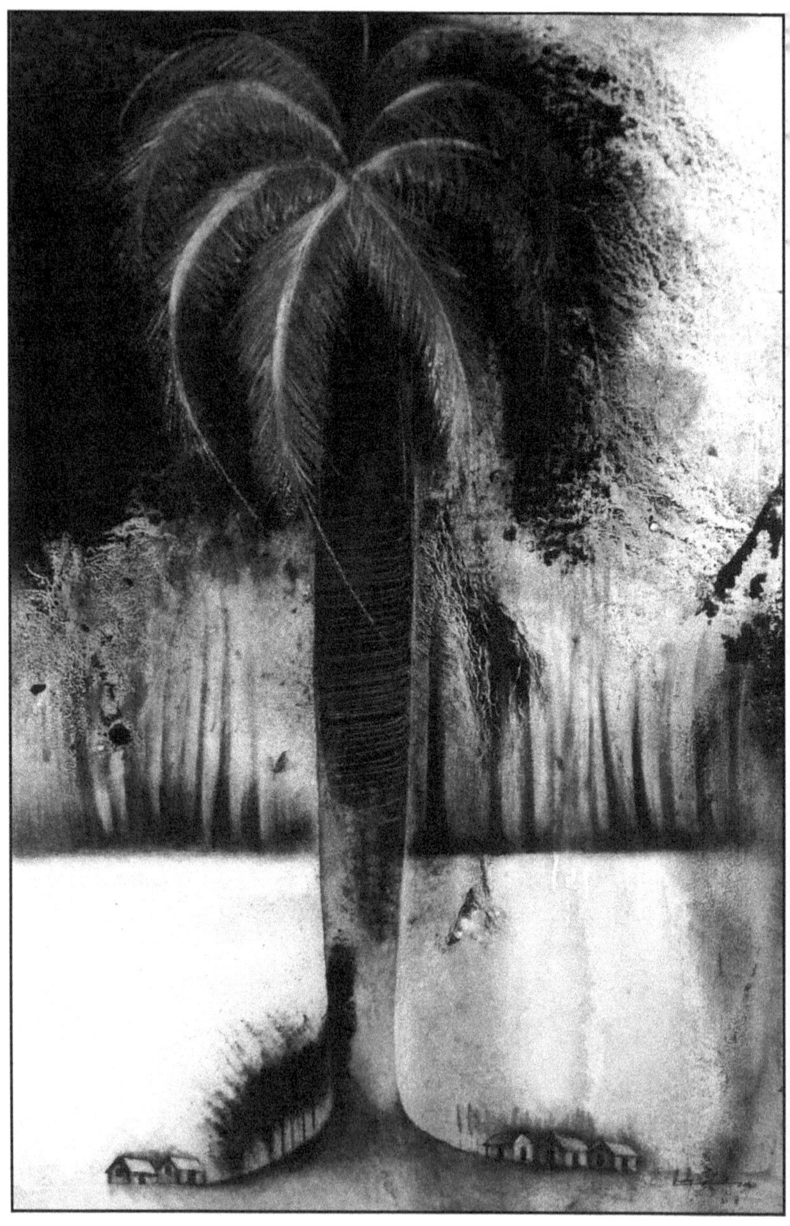

Through germination:
earth, water, sun once again
transform into seed.

发芽

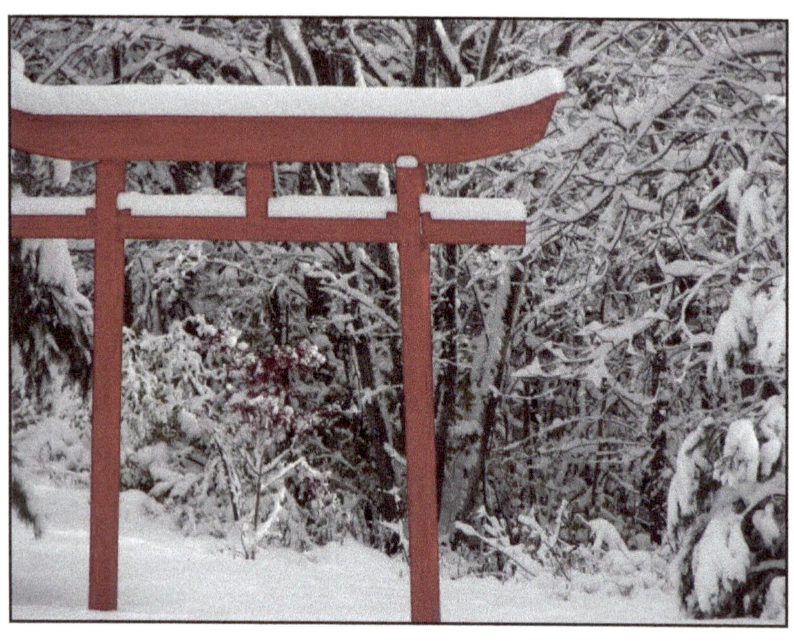

Behold green and white:
the Torii is red, as well,
and frames the maple.

フレーム

Life

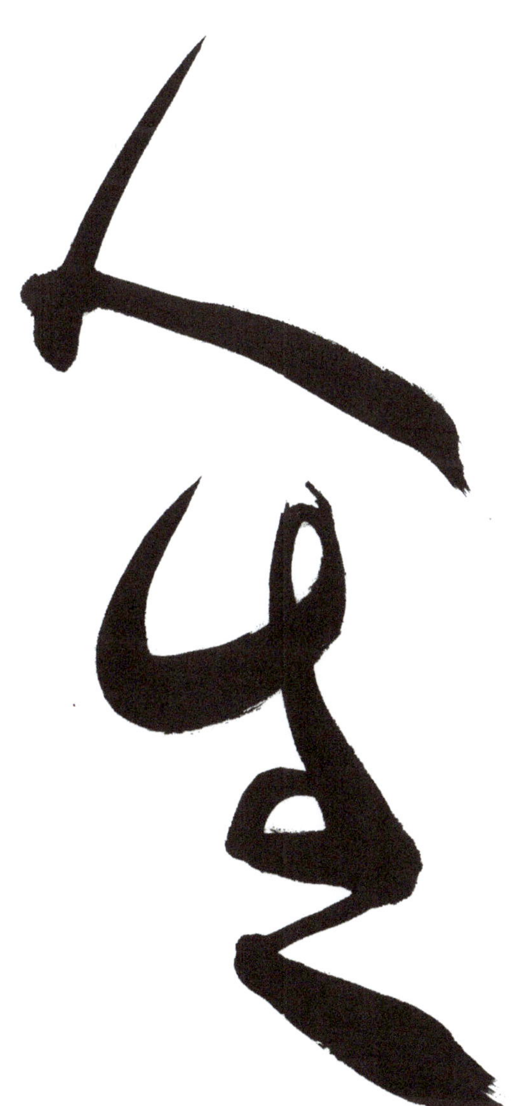

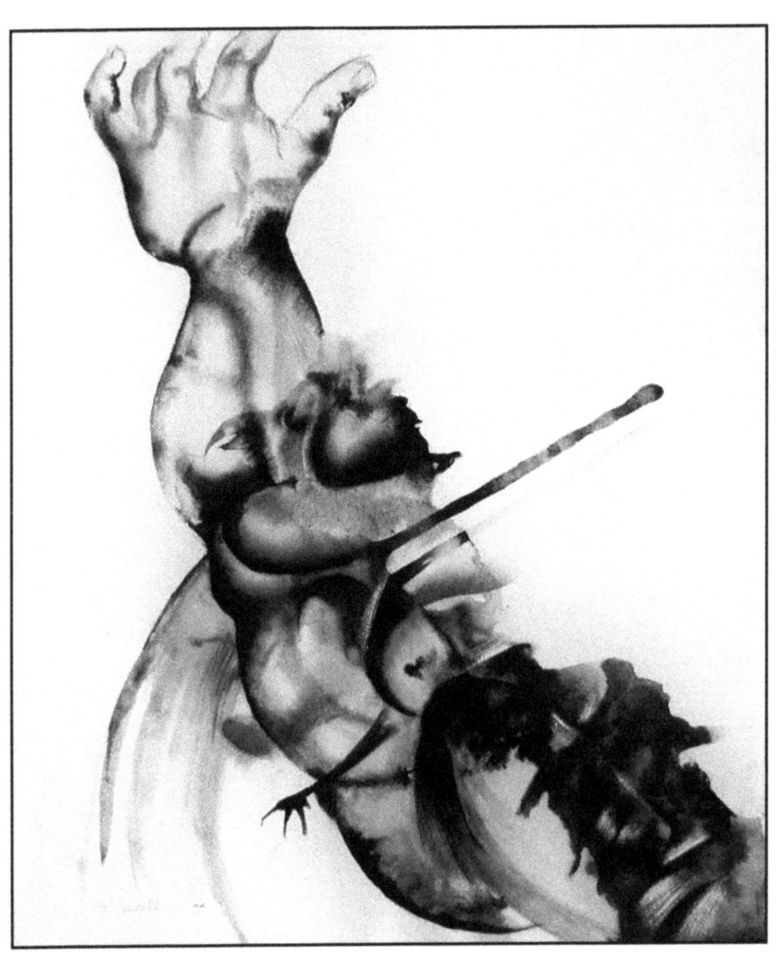

The skillful Master
with no bow, takes aim: and thud!
heron on the ground.

弓道

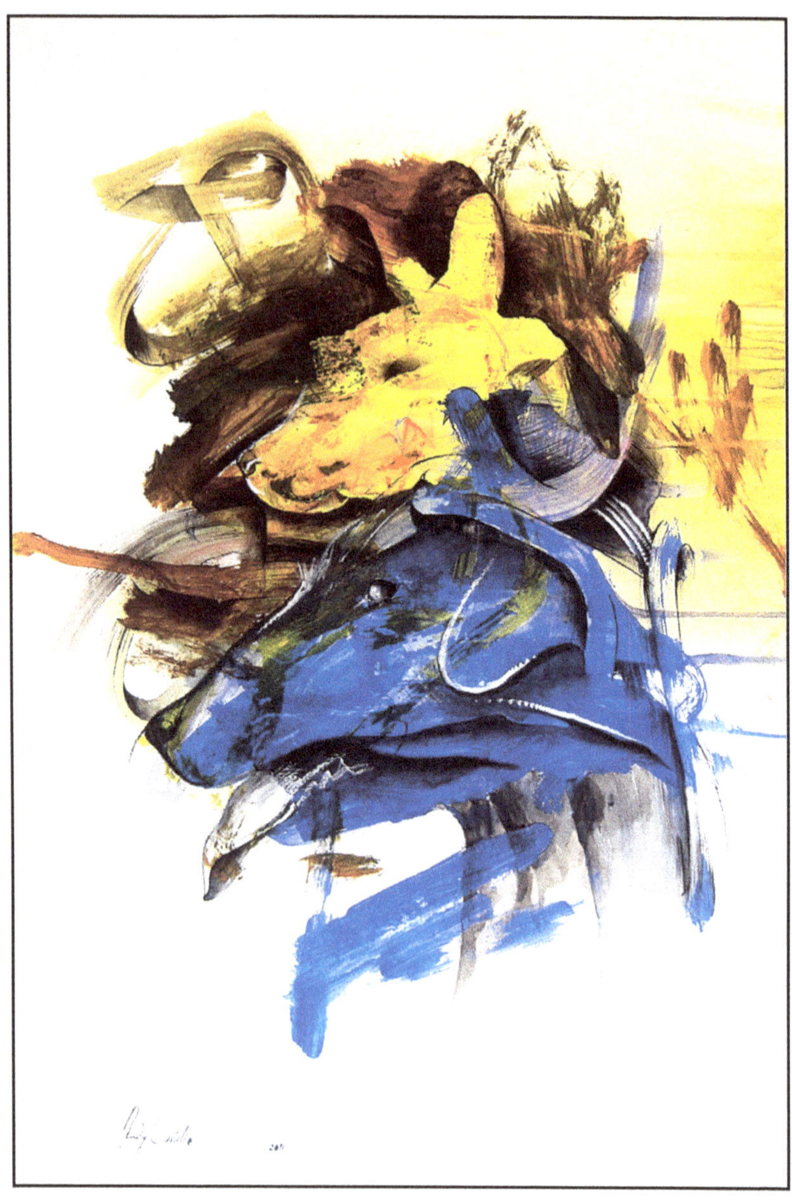

An unknown left hand
raises —a mirror— raises
a right hand unknown.

对

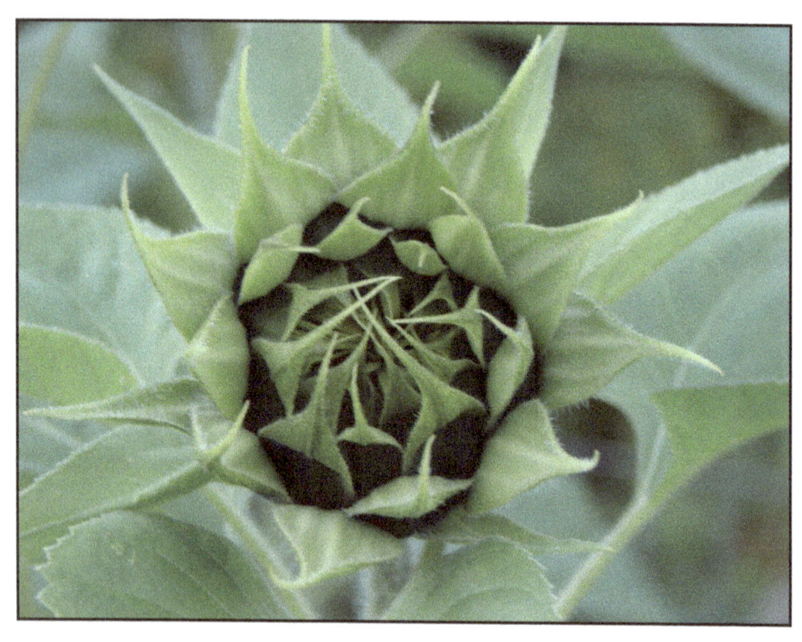

They were two before,
through procreation of one:
glad tidings and joy.

誕生

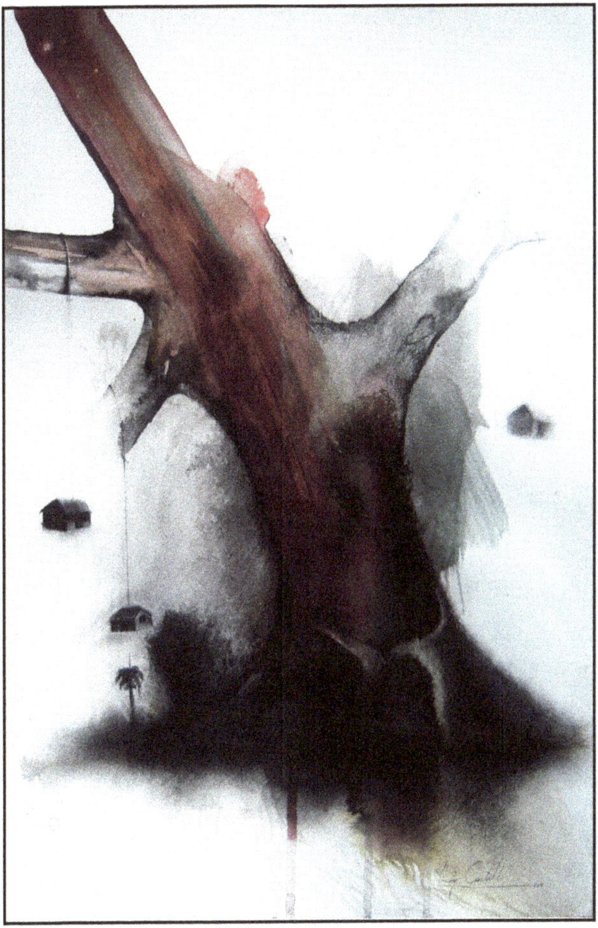

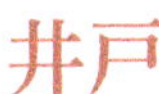

It's falling empty
into emptiness, it fills
and rises filled up.

井戸

47

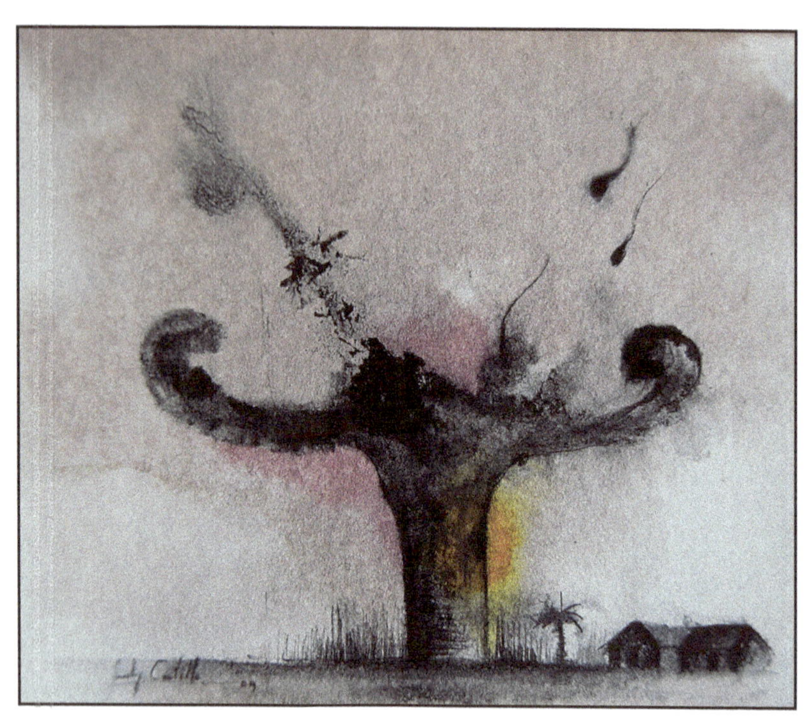

He's Emperor; yet,
in the Tea Ceremony:
mortal, as am I.

茶道

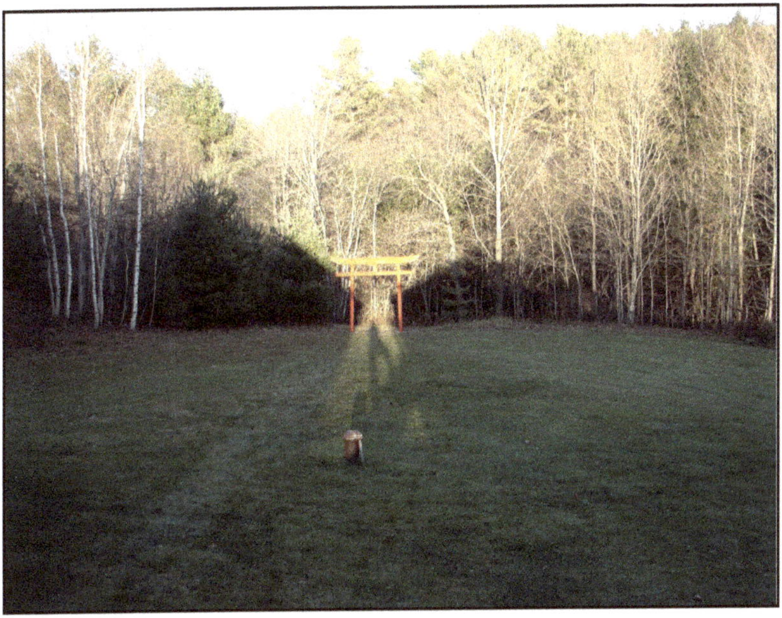

Kite's flight in the sun
tethers the boy to flying
and to his shadow.

糸

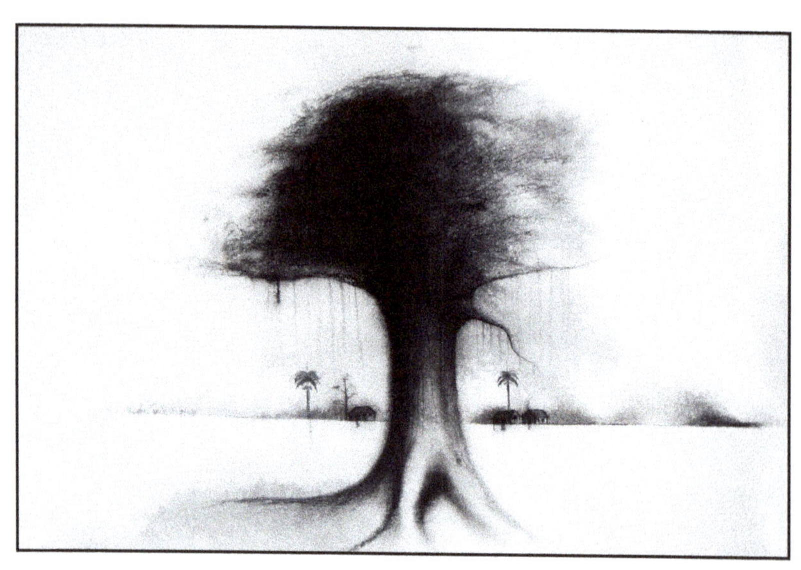

One so remembers
that which is forgotten; please:
don't remember me.

忘却

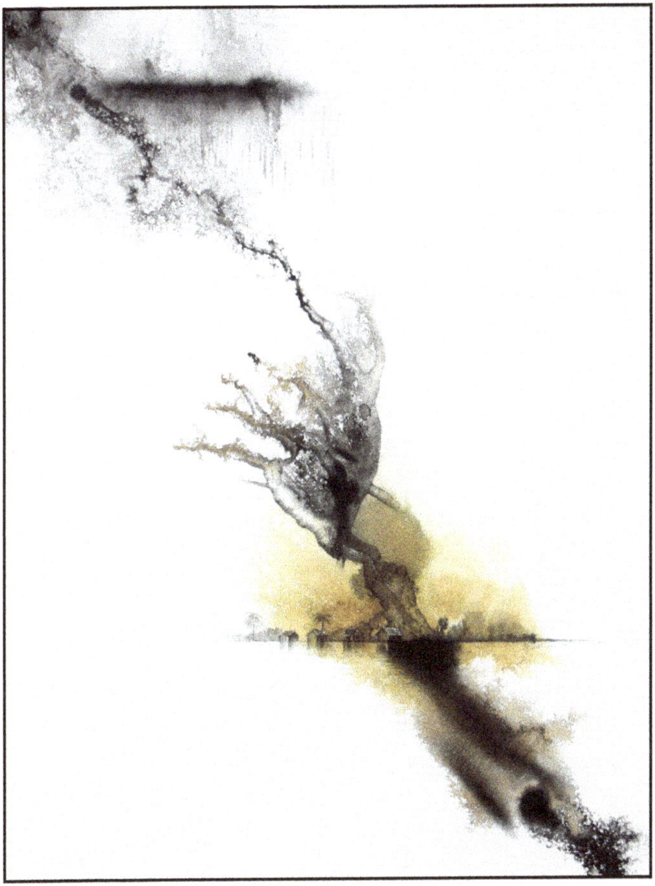

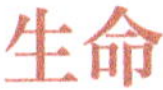

Descend and ascend
—passage on a two-way route—:
break of dawn—demise.

生命

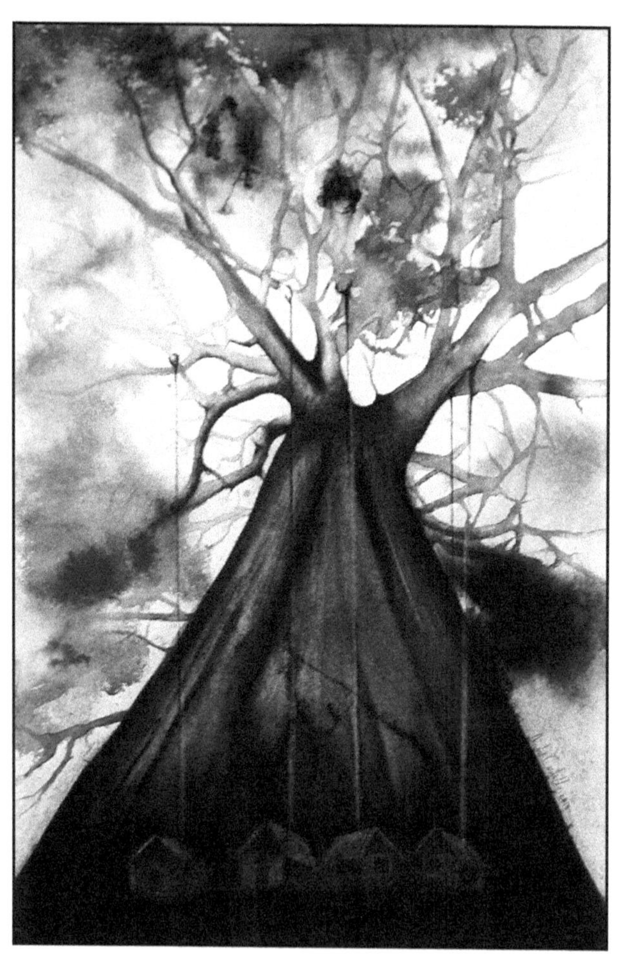

Bird made of paper
suspended by the drawstrings
of early childhood.

凧

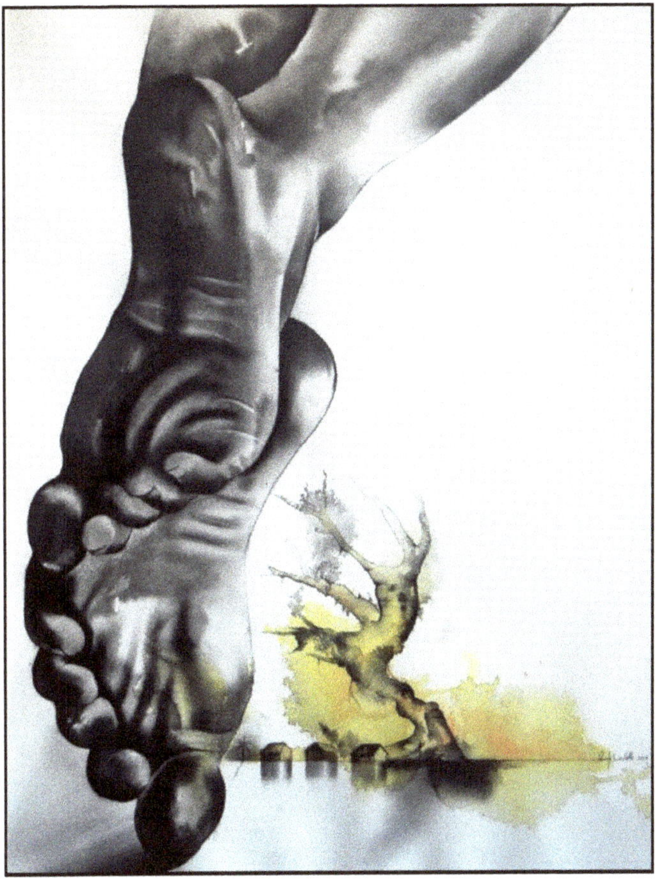

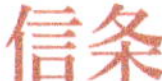

For reality
a daydreamer; and for dreams,
then, a realist.

信条

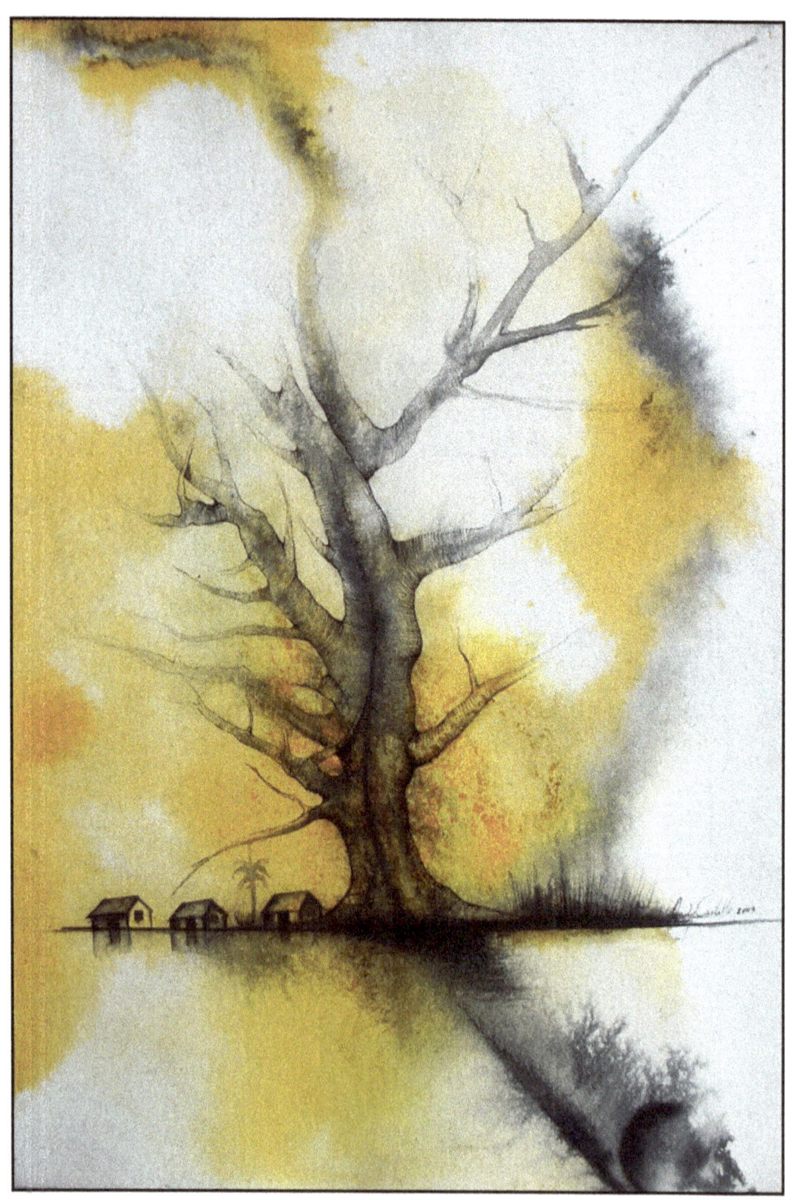

Today will be gone
tomorrow, and tomorrow
gone will be today.

時間

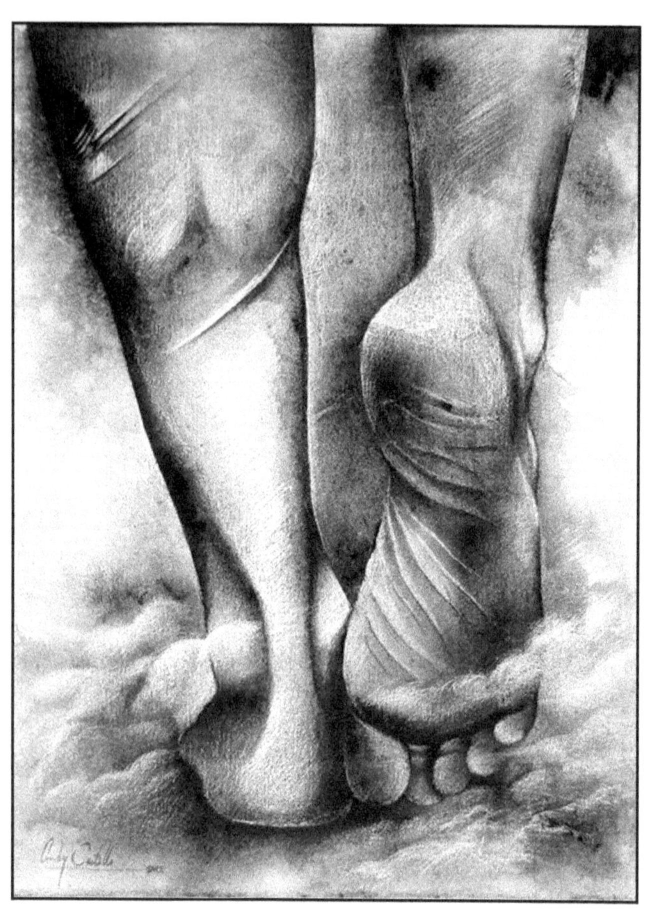

Fleeting arrivals
foreshadow the nostalgia
of lengthy partings.

出発

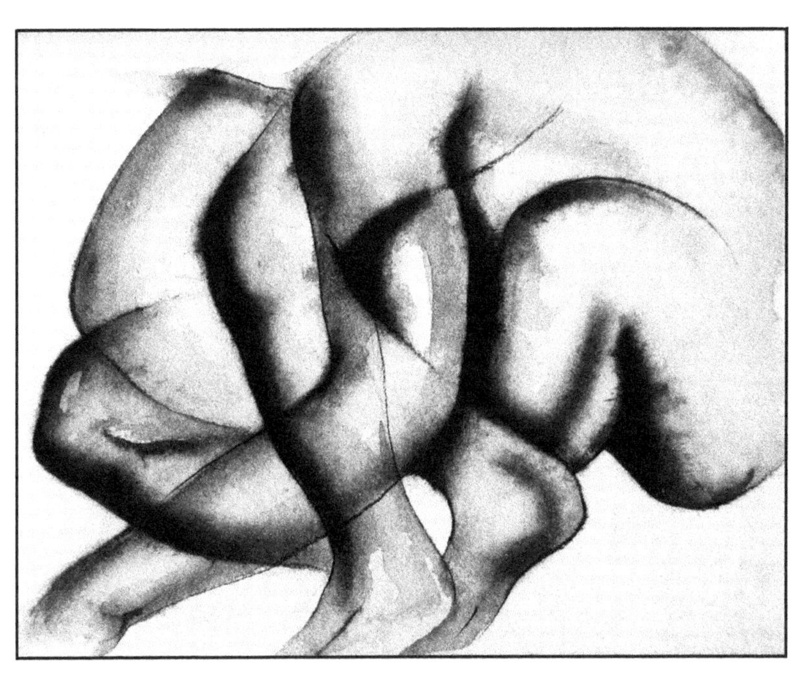

Donned on a torso
a kimono: one is dressed;
removed: one's naked.

人間

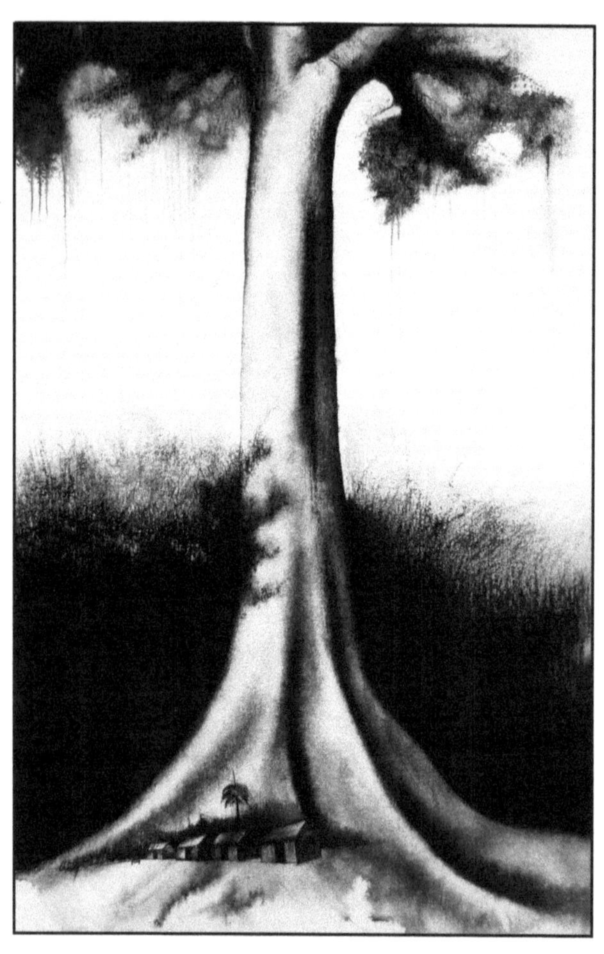

Oh, that what little
remains undone not ruin
all that came before.

調和

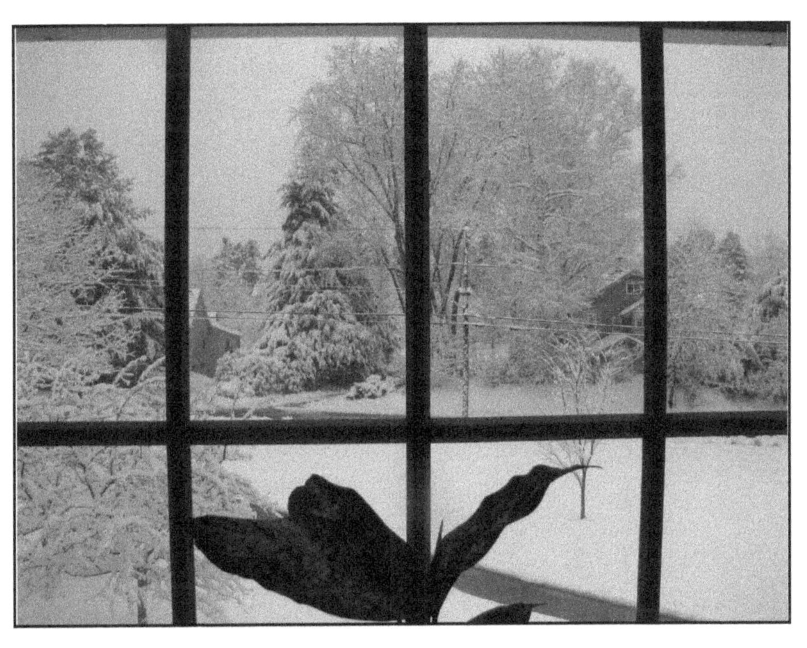

The air penetrates,
it is freeing me; today,
truly imprisoned.

仮出獄

Writing

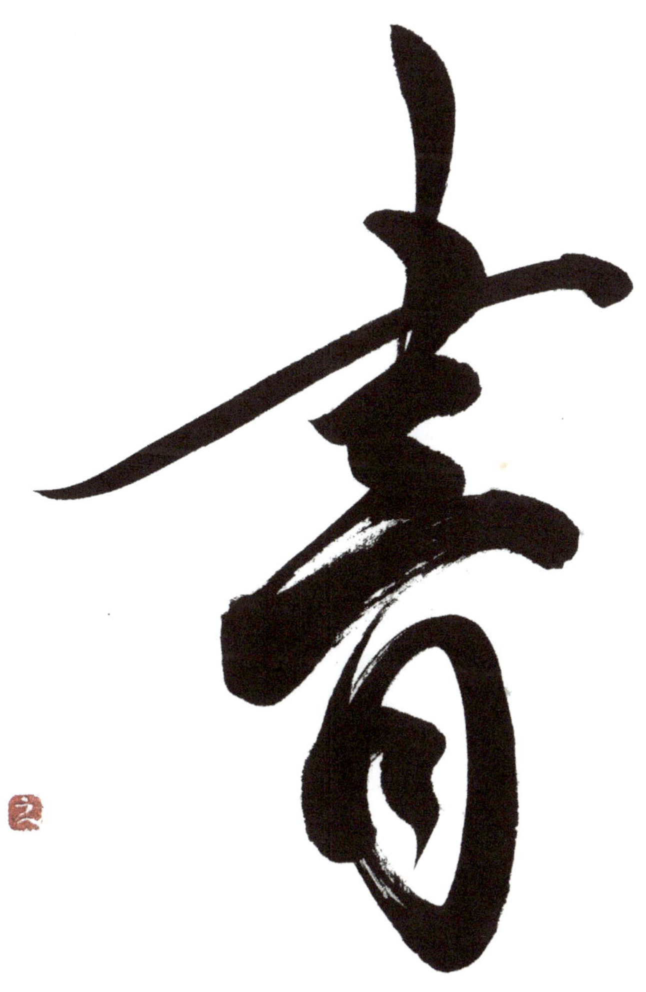

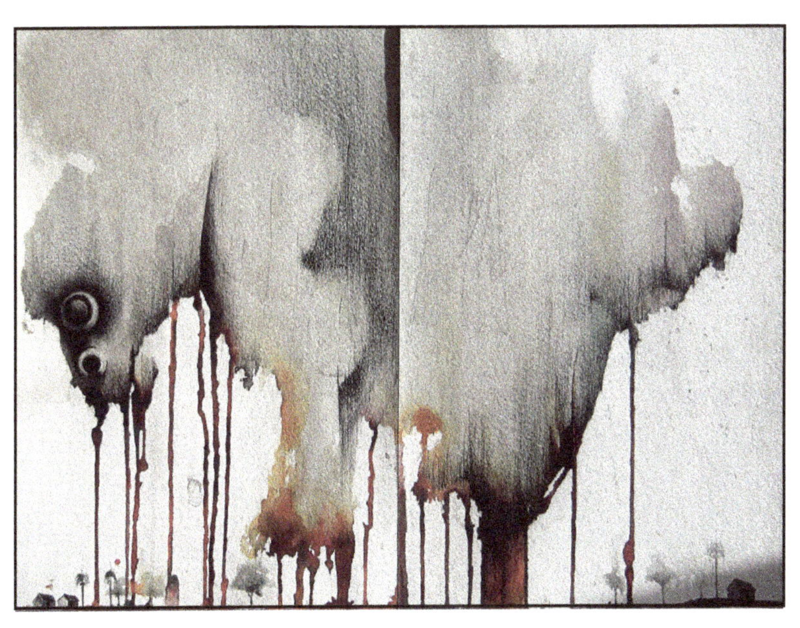

White is the paper,
I have not written it yet:
hence, there is still hope.

最後の詩

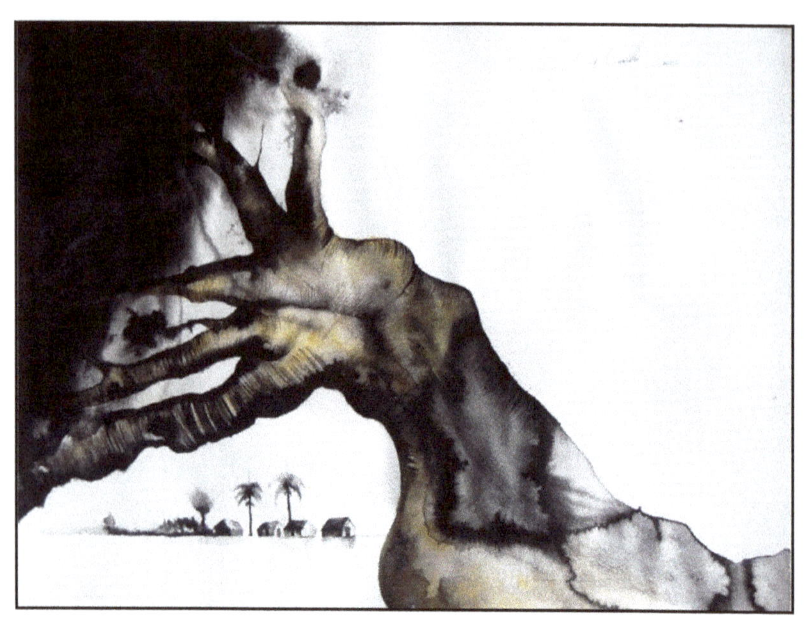

…and I have been here,
weeping such expectancy;
awaiting a verse.

待合室

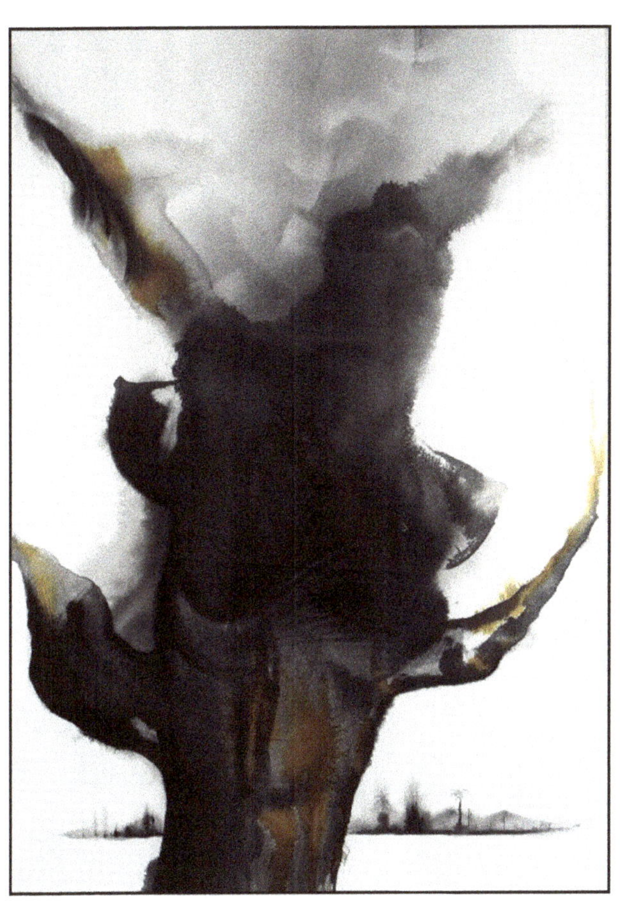

Whole entire verses
of disheveled images:
smudges without light.

不完全

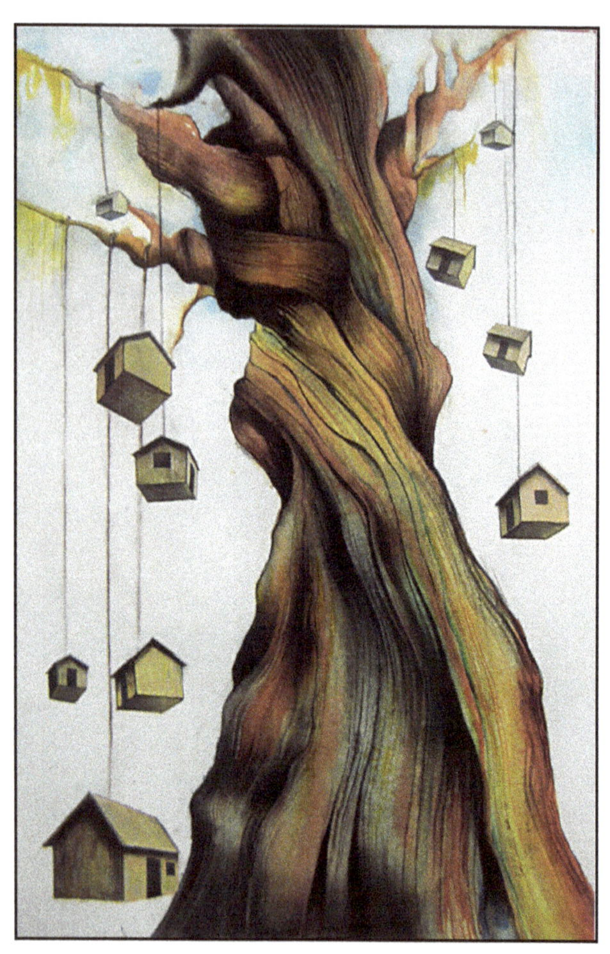

Playing creator,
everything was made to be
simply spectacle.

劇作家

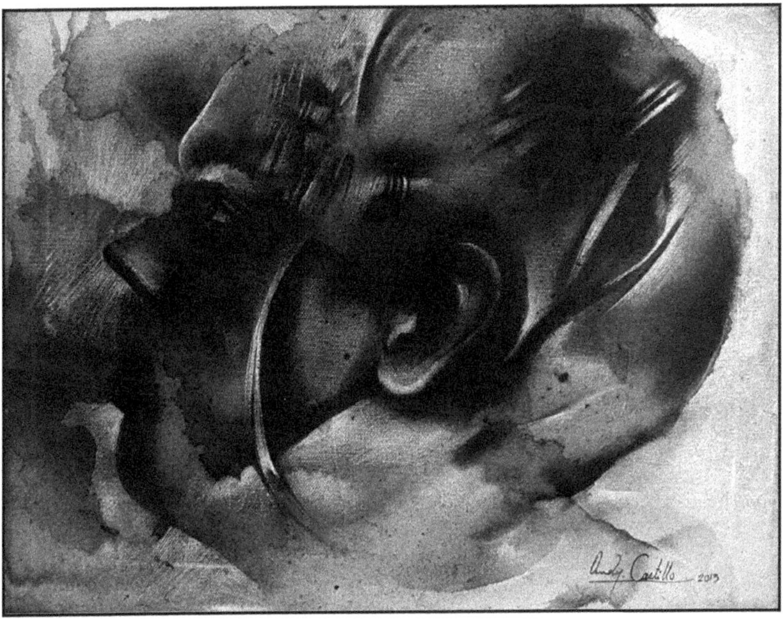

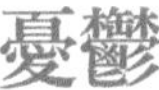

The kind of shadows
where one loses muses: when
engulfed by darkness.

憂鬱

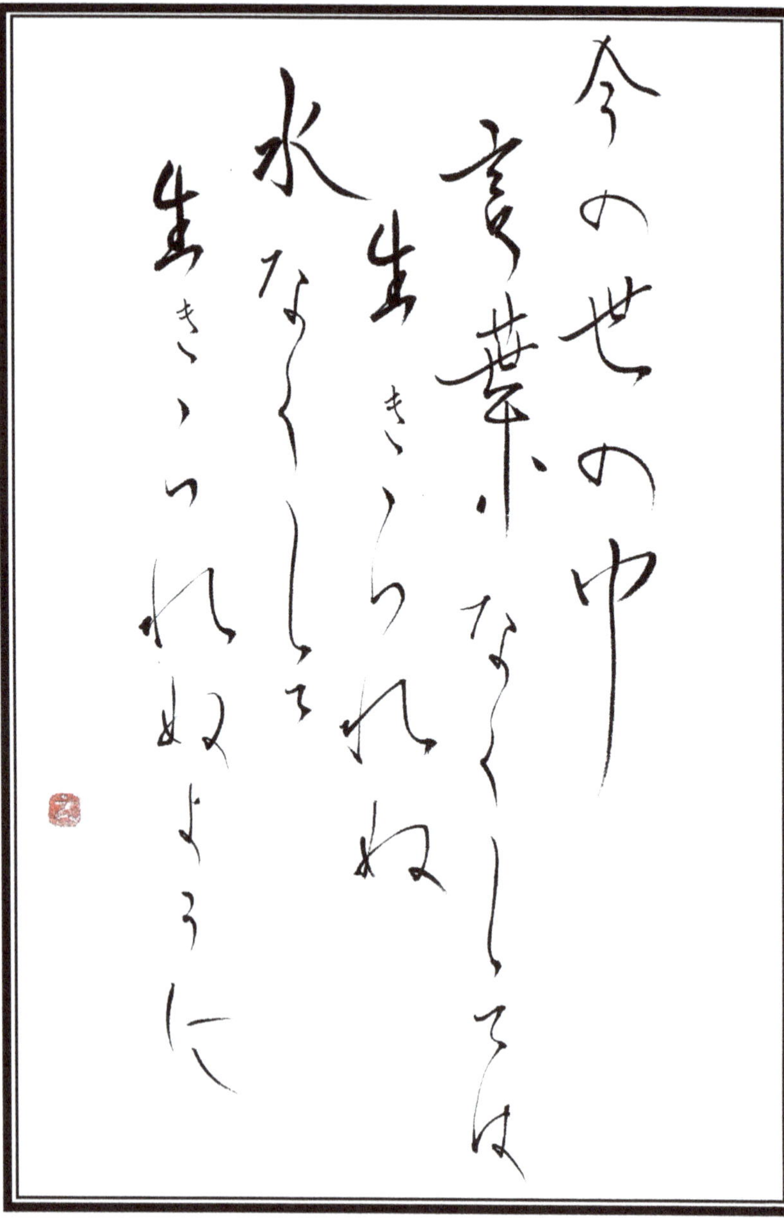

今の世の中
言葉なくしては
水生きられぬ
生きられぬように

Fine strokes of black ink
vociferating clear words
on a hung silk scroll.

掛け軸

On opposite page: Translation into Japanese by Akiko Harimoto "Soja" from Shodo Creativo (www.shodocreativo.com) of the haiku:
Today, without words, / it's impossible to live; / as without water

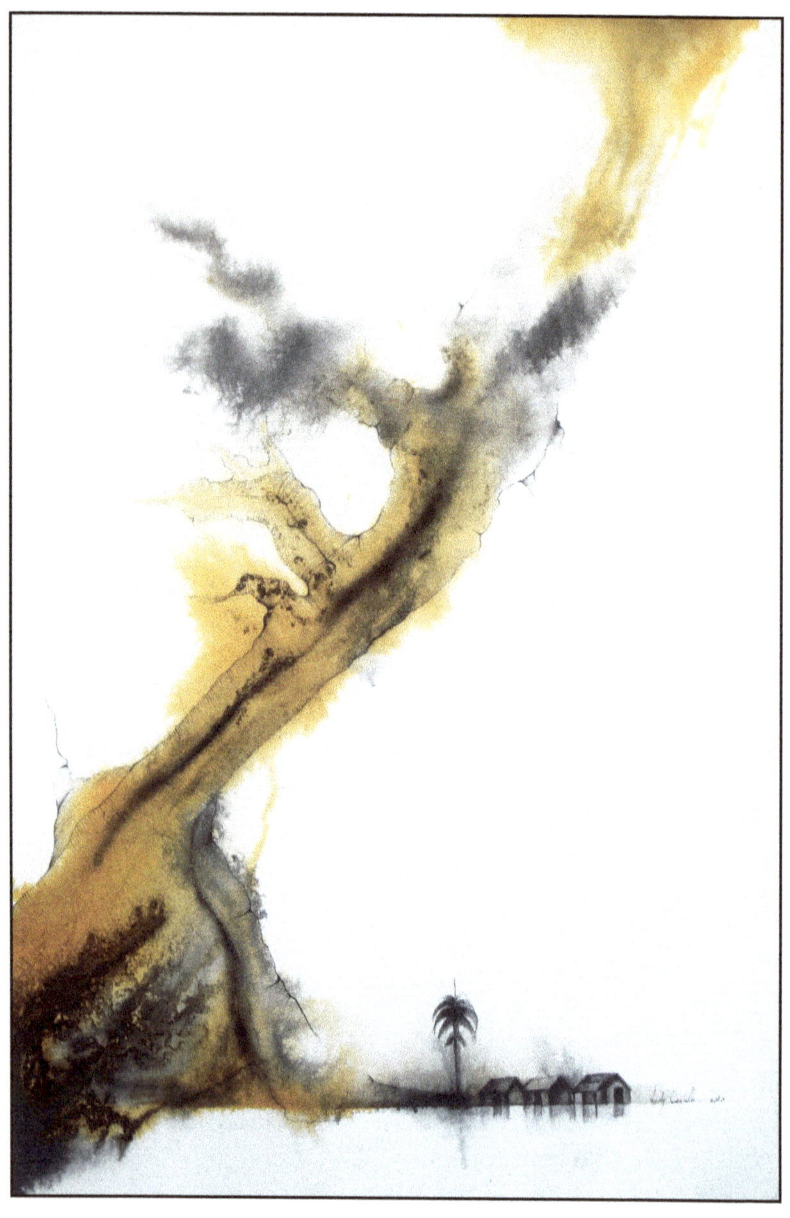

Today, without words,
it's impossible to live;
as without water.

真髄

Translator's Note

It would be appropriate to reiterate this and affirm that translation is a literary genre apart, different from the rest, with its own norms and own ends. The simple fact is that the translation is not the work, but a path toward the work. If this is a poetic work, the translation is no more than an apparatus, a technical device that brings us closer to the work without ever trying to repeat or replace it.

José Ortega y Gasset,
"The Misery and the Splendor of Translation"
Translation by Elizabeth Gamble Miller

When Keysi asked me to translate "Como el agua," I gave it considerable thought; translating poetry is difficult enough without having to adhere to the 5/7/5 syllable count particular to the haiku. After reading through the collection though, I was on board. Not only did I encounter miniature bursts of intensity of expression but a pictorial accompaniment carefully orchestrated to illuminate the verses. As I delved into my task, I found myself becoming a word detective —in so many instances Spanish words and their English equivalents have completely different syllabic counts. A challenge indeed, but in the end, a process similar to solving a puzzle whose pieces fit together in a new, dynamic way.

When we sat down to review the first draft, we read each haiku aloud —"en voz alta"— letting the words roll off our tongues. Sometimes they stuck on our palates and didn't flow quite as we had hoped, other times they flew into a magical space of their own. Keysi requested that the word *Torii*, which has three syllables in English and two syllables in its Spanish pronunciation, maintain its Spanish count; so we are counting it as a two-syllable word in this translation.

We continued editing until the "path toward the work" was cut. Like so many paths in Keysi's imagery, through maple trees, snow covered or bare, through sand and sea, through water coursing or frozen, a current runs from the Spanish to the English and back again. My hope is that the reader of this English translation is transported to Keysi's intimate world and, like water, is transformed along the way.

Elizabeth Polli
Naples, Florida, December 2016

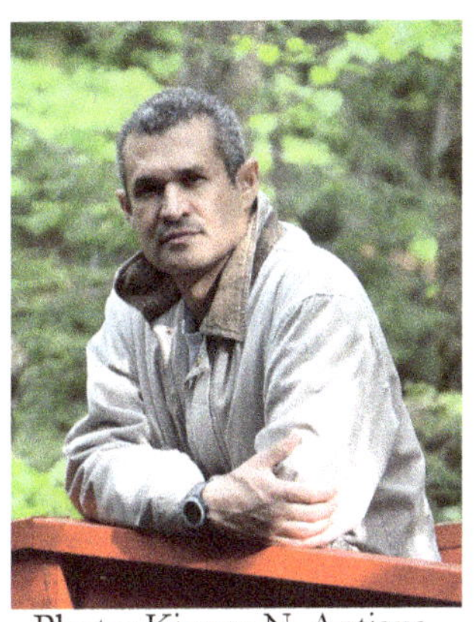

Photo: Kianny N. Antigua

Keiselim A. Montás

Santo Domingo, Dominican Republic, 1968; immigrated to the U.S. in 1985, where he completed high school, and went on to earn a BA & an MA in Spanish Language and Literatures.

He has published: *Pequeños Poemas Diurnos,* (chapbook of poems, 1992 & 2005); *Amor de ciudad grande* (poems, 2006); *Reminiscencias* (short stories, 2007); *Allá (diario del transtierro)* (poems, 2012; e-book 2013); *De la emigración al transtierro* (essays, 2015); *Como el agua (colección de Haikus)* (poems -haiku-, 2016); *Ínfimas apreciaciones literarias* (essays, 2016).

Included in: *Viajeros del rocío 25 narradores dominicanos de la diáspora* (anthology, 2008); *Nostalgias de Arena escritores de las comunidades dominicanas en EE.UU.* (anthology, 2011); *Shortstop microrrelatos de béisbol dominicano* (anthology, 2014); *The Americas Poetry Festival of New York 2014* (multilingual anthology, 2014); *The Americas Poetry Festival of New York 2016* (multilingual anthology, 2016); amongst others.

He has been awarded the following literary prizes: Third Prize "27th Annual Chicano/Latino Literary Prize," 2001 (poetry); Premio Letras de Ultramar 2006 (short story); Primer Lugar XIX Concurso de Cuentos Radio Santa María, 2012 (short story); Segundo Lugar, 2014 y Mención de Honor 2015, Premio de Cuento Juan Bosch (short story); Premio Letras de Ultramar 2015 (essay).

His blog: http://keiselimamontas.blogspot.com/

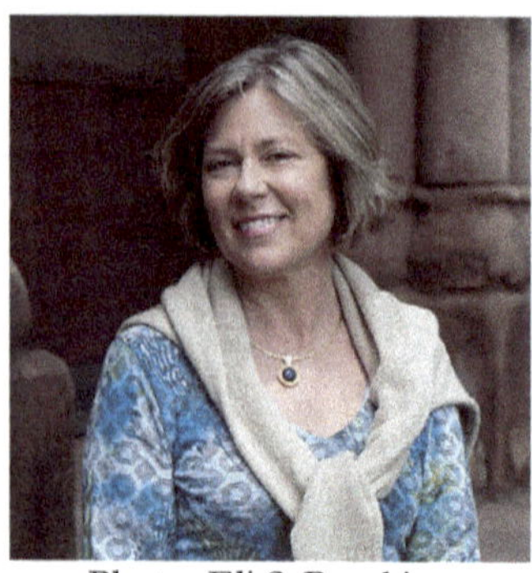

Photo: Eli S. Burakian

Elizabeth Polli

Taught Spanish language and literature, and was the Spanish Language Program Director at Dartmouth College from 1998 until 2014.

She began translating for the film industry in the 1980s, while in Spain. Her publications include translations of poetry, prose and essays by Sergio Chejfec, Felix de la Concha, Fritz Glockner, Ana Merino, José María Merino, Luis Muñoz and Wendy Guerra. Her translations of scholarly essays on comics have also appeared in the "International Journal of Comic Art." Elizabeth is also an avid knitter.

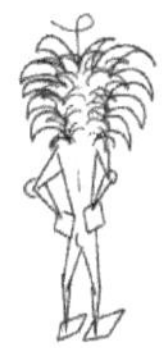

Zompopos
El libro es un Zompopo

Like Water (A Haiku Collection) by Keiselim A. Montás, translated from the Spanish by Elizabeth Polli, was completed in January 2017, in New Hampshire. This edition was finalized under the editorial care of the author.

Other books by The Zompopos Project:

Amor de ciudad grande (Poems, 2006)

Allá (diario del transtierro) (Poems, 2012)

Cuando el resto se apaga (Poems, 2013)

Islamabad queda al norte (Poems, 2014)

En sus pupilas una luna a punto de madurar (Poems, 2015)

Como el agua (colección de Haikus) (Poems, 2016)

All available at: http://editorialzompopos.blogspot.com/

The Zompopos Project: This Project champions the Zompopo (*leaf cutting ant / atta cephalotes*) as a symbol of cooperation amongst humans and our living environment by finding common ground via needs, culture, language and ideals. It proposes a look at our daily lives and a revision of our modes of consumption in order to find uses for objects we would normally discard.

El Proyecto Zompopos: Este proyecto promulga al Zompopo (*hormiga corta hojas / atta cephalotes*) como un símbolo de cooperación entre los humanos y nuestro medio ambiente, identificando intereses comunes en necesidades, cultura, lenguaje e ideales. Propone un auto-examen de nuestra cotidianidad y una revisión de nuestras formas de consumo para dar nuevos usos a objetos que normalmente desechamos.

www.ingramcontent.com/pod-product-compliance
Lightning Source LLC
Chambersburg PA
CBHW050035040726
47599CB00015B/1687